Josette Baer (ed)

The Seven Deadly Sins 3.0

A Liberal Critique of the Contemporary Lack of Ethics and
Rationalism in Science, Society, and Politics in the Third Millennium

T0247622

Josette Baer (ed)

THE SEVEN DEADLY SINS 3.0
A Liberal Critique of the Contemporary Lack of Ethics and
Rationalism in Science, Society, and Politics in the
Third Millennium

ibidem
Verlag

Bibliographic information published by the Deutsche Nationalbibliothek

Die Deutsche Nationalbibliothek lists this publication in the Deutsche Nationalbibliografie; detailed bibliographic data are available on the Internet at http://dnb.d-nb.de.

Bibliografische Information der Deutschen Nationalbibliothek

Die Deutsche Nationalbibliothek verzeichnet diese Publikation in der Deutschen Nationalbibliografie; detaillierte bibliografische Daten sind im Internet über http://dnb.d-nb.de abrufbar.

ISBN-13: 978-3-8382-1642-3

© *ibidem*-Verlag, Hannover • Stuttgart 2024

All rights reserved.

No part of this publication may be reproduced, stored in or introduced into a retrieval system, or transmitted, in any form, or by any means (electronic, mechanical, photocopying, recording or otherwise) without the prior written permission of the publisher. Any person who commits any unauthorized act in relation to this publication may be liable to criminal prosecution and civil claims for damages.

Alle Rechte vorbehalten. Das Werk einschließlich aller seiner Teile ist urheberrechtlich geschützt. Jede Verwertung außerhalb der engen Grenzen des Urheberrechtsgesetzes ist ohne Zustimmung des Verlages unzulässig und strafbar. Dies gilt insbesondere für Vervielfältigungen, Übersetzungen, Mikroverfilmungen und elektronische Speicherformen sowie die Einspeicherung und Verarbeitung in elektronischen Systemen.

Printed in the United States of America

Table of Contents

Acknowledgements

The idea for this book emerged in the last months of 2020 when I was working on a biography of Slovak dissident Hana Ponická,[1] a true heroine who had stood up for freedom of speech against the Communist Czechoslovak government in the 1970s and 1980s. Her outspoken protest brought upon her the cruel wrath of those wielding power in a totalitarian regime. The infamous Czechoslovak State Security Service exercised all possible means of psychological torture and intimidation, but they could not silence an elderly and courageous lady. I looked at the historical details of Communist Czechoslovakia, especially the state-controlled media that presented a different reality to the citizens: the Communist Party believed that since 1948 Slovaks and Czechs lived in the best social and political system mankind had ever created. Those who dared to differ and said so in public were mercilessly persecuted and punished with imprisonment. Freedom of speech was an unrealistic dream in Communist Czechoslovakia.

When the world was in the first coronavirus lockdown in 2020, and later when the first wave of vaccination was organized in my country, I wondered why I was so confused by the contradictory information about vaccines we citizens were and are still receiving. Inspired by my confusion about the news and the role traditional and social media play in our

---

[1]   Josette Baer, *The Green Butterfly. Hana Ponická (1922–2007, Slovak Writer, Poetess and Dissident* (Stuttgart, New York: ibidem, Columbia University Press), 2022.

7

lives, namely the question of which news channels one could trust, I decided to address this theme with a book and invited colleagues and friends to contribute. Our aim is to present to the reader our views of the times we live in: what makes living in the third millennium so special, compared to the 1990s or the early 2000s?

Just think about how technology has advanced since the mid-1990s: mobile phones, smart phones, the internet, laptops and online banking, internet shops, an enhanced online credit card system, and lastly, social media such as Facebook, TikTok, Twitter and Instagram, which affect especially the younger generation's way of communicating and receiving news. My generation grew up writing letters to our friends or calling them on our parents' landline, but we had a rich social life. Once we all had mobile phones, keeping in touch with friends became so much easier.

Thinking about how I would organize such a publication, one night, I dreamt of the title: The Seven Deadly Sins 3.0, referring to our third millennium and what we might consider a sin in our times, thereby inquiring about the moral values and ethical norms of our societies and how they affect citizens' lives. My friends and colleagues immediately replied to my call. I had asked them to pick a sin from the catalogue of sins based on the summary by James Stalker.[2] Stalker, a Baptist pastor, summarized the seven deadly sins with the scholastic catchword SALIGIA: Superbia = Pride, Avaritia = Avarice,

---

[2]   James Stalker, D.D. *The Seven Deadly Sins* (Printed in Poland: Forgotten Books, 2012). The original book was published in London by Hodder & Stoughton in 1901 or 1902.

Luxuria = Luxury, Invidia = Envy, Gula = Appetite, Ira = Anger and Accidia = Sloth.[3]

As a Swiss citizen, I grew up with Western values: freedom of speech, direct democracy, and a deep admiration for the US constitution. As a liberal, I cherish civil and political rights, an open and tolerant society, a free market economy, and I do not want the state meddling in my private life.

Not only in private discussions with friends, but also as a teacher, I think that an open, respectful, and rational debate is still a moral value we should pursue. The Roman saying *audiatur et altera pars* (listen also to the other side) is one of the pillars of an open and tolerant society and the Roman legal system. I had ample opportunity to experience authoritarian and totalitarian regimes, owing to my profession as a scholar. I vividly remember citizens' anxious and timid faces in the Minsk metro on a daily basis. And the Russian habit of displaying a neutral, emotionless face when in public to avoid drawing the attention of the authorities to oneself, which we in the West interpret as rude, arrogant, and unfriendly behaviour. Russians never smile in public. Why? Stalinism taught them not to stand out with a smile in public. I also remember the deep mistrust of East Europeans towards tourists and foreigners who are free to leave the country if they do not like where they are living; that right of individual mobility was not bestowed on citizens in Communist Eastern Europe. They could not even decide to move house; the Communist governments told them what to do and what not to do. State-controlled news media reported only one side of a

---

[3]   Stalker, preface.

complex international situation, and, lastly, the terrible economic situation after the Soviet system of planned economy collapsed in 1991 affected everyone. This collapse of enormous proportions forced many East Europeans to emigrate to the West in the 1990s. I also experienced how the lack of alternative information broadcast by the Belarusian state media affected my mind and critical faculties when I lived in Minsk for a year.

Now, our journey has reached its destination, and we are very happy with the result. We would like to thank Christian Schön at ibidem Verlag for his kind and professional support. We, the authors of this book, value our friendship; we often disagree during our regular Zoom meetings but respect the different views held. One could call us a college of friends who like to disagree and debate.

Peter Thomas Hill is the author of the prologue, a bemused look at life as we know it. Peter has also copy-edited all the texts written by authors who are not native English speakers. Jabbar Moradi's contribution deals with pride in science; he questions the arrogance of scientists, and how science has been changing our understanding of objectivity and facts. Pavle Krsmanović investigates the ethical problem of trust in science, inquiring about intellectual sloth, the idleness over thinking things through as a coping mechanism during the COVID-19 pandemic. Katarzyna Suboticki deals with the sin of appetite, analysing the trends of fat-shaming and body positivity. Slovakia's best-selling author Jozef Banáš's epilogue addresses in a humoristic and self-critical way the seven deadly sins the Slovak nation is guilty of. Lastly, I hope that my contributions on avarice, envy and anger-hate complement our impressions of life in the third millennium.

A last word on sins: naturally, we authors do not conceive of the word 'sin' in the way Reverend Stalker did, i.e. defending a distinct Christian view of the world and its strict moral prescriptions. Indeed, all seven sins are not deadly for the individual, neither had they been deadly when Stalker explained them to his readers in the early 20th century. 'Sin' is, in Stalker's interpretation, a moral guide in the sense of what not to do in your life; it should be understood in an abstract version, not as original sin. So, why are they then referred to as deadly? We think because of one reason: they are deadly to societal cohesion, citizens' psychological well-being and a peaceful and open society.

Let me explain why: If, for example, I am gay, I do not have to be afraid of ending up in prison, as Irish author Oscar Wilde (1854–1900) had to endure in the 19th century. No government in the free West can imprison me for my sexual orientation. Neither do I have to fear my teacher's punishment when I am a lazy student. If I love my food and eat so much that I become obese, my doctor will warn me about the dangers, but in a free society, I am free to choose my poisons, my lifestyle, even if they are killing me.

We understand The Seven Deadly Sins as follows: they originate in Christian moral thought and still have some validity in our digital societies today. They are 'sins' because they, as we think, affect the fabric of society by means of deadly diversity. Any functioning society requires a measure of cohesion to keep the state and civil rights functional. Once bad behaviour and wrong choices are accepted as the norm, a free and open society collapses, doomed by means of its own liberty and tolerance of toxic sociopathic behaviour.

If a court declares me the victim, while all evidence proves that I am the criminal perpetrator, justice and the legal system have become dysfunctional. If obesity is the new norm, if people believe, against all medical research and knowledge, that one can weigh 300 pounds and still be healthy, the costs of healthcare systems will skyrocket, and they will eventually collapse. In fact, this is happening as we speak. If arrogance in scientific research is the norm, society can no longer question government policies in education and technology, and if sloth or laziness as a way of not coping with problems is widely accepted, we are giving up our civil liberties to question those in power. If I hate a certain nation or minority just because they have different cultural traditions, I endanger the future of international peace and cooperation, and if I am guided by envy, I forsake the opportunity to learn and improve my financial and educational situation. If I am wealthy and tight-fisted, my greed hurts those who are in need, and my avarice makes me look with contempt at those in need, without understanding that it is not always their fault when fate deals them a cruel blow. A humanistic society strives to integrate all its citizens, to help those in need, support the weak and establish equality of access to education.

If we overindulge in our wishes and pursue these 'sins' as behavioural and lifestyle choices, they will affect the openness and tolerance of our societies, which are based on three pillars: economic prosperity, that is Capitalism that runs according to its own rules, the rule-of-law state, and science promoted and undertaken by researchers. We think that these three pillars should be protected and promoted; once they are gone, we are back to pre-modern behaviour, believing in shamanism or the weather gods, and having to endure the usurpation of political power by a political elite we did not elect. Conspiracy theories are just that: people with a lot of imagination are trying to explain the inexplicable in their own way. Yet, if members of the tin-foil-hat brigade were in power, we would be catapulted back to the Middle Ages, in intellectual and scientific terms.

Lastly, we authors would be more than happy if our little book could open a debate about deadly sins in our third millennium.

Josette Baer
Zurich, February 2024

PROLOGUE

In the beginning was the word and the word was God. And man created God in his own image, in the image of man created he Him. Hmm, I don't think so ... not the first phrase, anyway. By the time words and language evolved, about half of human history had passed.

Fiat lux

'Let there be light.' *Fiat lux* is not a high-end model from the Italian car marque, but an evocative phrase from Genesis.[1] Paraphrasing the Bible and Genesis seems a good place to start talking sin. The role of a prologue is to get the book that follows in perspective. Context, then text.

Lifespan[2]

Picture the history and pre-history of the human species as a 5ft walking staff, the approximate altitude of the brain after *Homo erectus* started standing up for himself.

Now, imagine a metal ferrule about two inches long at the tip of the staff. This band marks the past 10,000 years (10 ka), a hundred or

---

[1]   Latin translation of the biblical Hebrew יְהִי אוֹר (yehi 'or). Church Latin has outlived Mortal Sin.

[2]   *The Archdeacon*, by Ilya Repin (1844-1930): https://commons.wikimedia.org/wiki/File:Archdeacon_by_Repin.jpg, accessed 23 February 2023.

so centuries measured against the entire span of human life (some 300 ka).

We know something of the archaic past thanks to pioneering work in archaeology, anthropology and cognitive science.[3] Archaic humans ranged across the wilderness of the deep past, hunting and gathering, following the game and the seasons. Their simple, modular minds evolved, through a process known as cognitive fluidity, into the modern human imagination, with all the riches of original thought, analogy, metaphor, poetry and humour—the product of brains capable of powerful reasoning, as well as inspiration and lateral thinking.[4]

The primitive existence of prehistoric nomads evolved into a largely sedentary, civilized society, enabling the development of agriculture from around 10,000 years ago, and then in the past 5,000 years of recorded history, social progress, science, culture and the arts.[5] One inch on the staff of life.

---

[3]   In his brilliant, groundbreaking book *The Prehistory of the Mind*, Professor Steven Mithen of Reading University (UK), postulates that the point at which humans distinguished themselves from the rest of the animal kingdom was when their brains developed the ability to think in metaphors, to conceptualize, to express abstract thoughts.

[4]   Einstein was not the only pebble on the beach.

[5]   These are broad-brush figures. Surviving cave art bears witness to the prehistoric origins of the artistic impulse, at least as long ago as 40 or 50,000 years. My guide is a rule of thumb, given that the ferrule on the Archdeacon's staff is about the length of my thumb.

Post lucem tenebrae

Most of history is unknown and unknowable. What is written down, broadcast, or told and retold in oral history is a tiny fraction of the stories unfolding around us and around the world, now and in the past. Untold history is like the dark matter of human life.

The Dark Ages

The great civilizations of the Ancient World, of China, India, Persia and Egypt, preceded the European empires of antiquity: Greece and Rome. The decline and fall of the Roman Empire[6] gave way to the Dark Ages, a thousand years of cruelty, oppression, and organized religion.

The Enlightenment and the dawn of modernity, the triumph of science over superstition, gave rise to a desire for freedom and equality that was expressed in seminal events such as the American War of Independence and a generation later the French Revolution. These touchstones were counterpoints to the Age of Empire, which dominated four centuries of European and world history.

The Age of Empire

The British established hegemony over much of the Earth's surface by force of the East India Company, the opium trade, pirates such as Sir Francis Drake, and the might of the Royal

---

[6] *The Decline and Fall of the Roman Empire*, Edward Gibbon, an abridgement by D. M. Low, Chatto and Windus, London, 1978.

Navy. After the turn of the long 19th century (1789-1914),[7] the Age of Empire came to a bloody end in the First World War, and the horrors of 20th-century totalitarianism broke upon us. Now, again, we live in dark times—or rather, we live in dim times.

The Dim Ages

We live in a time when nearly half the US electorate[8] willingly puts its trust in a tall man who wears platform shoes. We live in a time of truth decay and mettle fatigue: The Dim Ages.

Capital sins

The Seven Deadly Sins, which became part of the Christian canon in the 6th century, are no longer relevant in the world I inhabit, the godless world of enlightened atheism and science. I and my kindred spirits do not recognize divine law, so how can we transgress against it? I live in a minority that is godless. Many more people are under the sway of one or other of the monotheistic religions. For those poor souls, perhaps, Deadly Sin is still capitalized.

---

[7]   British historian Eric Hobsbawm (1917-2012) and Russian writer Ilya Ehrenburg (1891-1967) coined the phrase 'the long nineteenth century' for the period from 1789 to 1914. Eric Hobsbawm: *The Age of Revolution: Europe 1789–1848* (Weidenfeld & Nicolson, 1962).

[8]   The United States of America is the *fons et origo* of liberal democracy, the founding father of the modern world; sadly, now on the watchlist.

Brand story

The original Deadly Sins were proclaimed by the mediaeval Church,[9] the most successful global brand in history. Having established the overriding moral framework and underlying culture of sin, punishment and redemption, the Church went

Kingdom come[10]

a step further by creating at least one highly lucrative business model based on it: the monetization of guilt, also known as indulgences. Guilt is to the religious what grass is to sheep. To reinforce the message and ensure obedience, the Church, through its Inquisition, and the successive governments of

---

9   The Catholic Church is one of the arithmetical religions that grows largely by multiplication rather than addition.

10   *The Harrowing of Hell*, Jacob van Swanenburg: https://en.wikiped ia.org/wiki/File:Jacob_van_Swanenburg_–The_Harrowing_of_Hell. jpg, accessed 6 April 2023.

states across Europe, both Catholic and Protestant, staged public trials, torture and executions of scarcely imaginable cruelty. Who could doubt the torments of Hell awaiting sinners when they were enacted on public squares?

Similar models were built by other monotheistic, authoritarian faiths, though none, I think, as cruel and inhumane as Christian practices in the Middle Ages, and none offering entertainment in the form of audiovisual presentations as elaborate as ritual Christian torture and killing. The public execution of dissidents and those guilty of apostasy in certain Muslim countries to this day comes a distant second.

Fiat lux, panem et circenses

'Let there be light entertainment.' Historically, Pompei's circus in Rome presented popular entertainments in which slaves and captives were murdered on stage—an ancient forerunner of snuff movies—but these were mere amusements, not instructional.

Backbone

Freethinkers face the daunting task of making up their own integrity. To lead a morally upright life, lacking the exoskeleton of religious morality, we have to grow our own spine, strong and true. A notable fact, which is in no way paradoxical, is that I regard the more enlightened believers in religions of every stamp as close confederates. They are selfless in their devotion to others. Their lives and beliefs are different, but their actions and attitudes similar. Purely contemplative beliefs such as Buddhism likewise share, through their spirituality and wisdom, the mindset of selflessness that is the beating heart and lifeblood of a free and democratic society.

Candide camera

What of the deadly sins today—the theme of this book? As a time-traveller   from the 20th century, I find myself marooned in the 21st, beyond hope of rescue, clutching at straws in the rising flood of conformism and anomie: people pleasing themselves, into their tiny minds—if not out of them.

But fear not, visionary plutocrats worlds apart are building spaceships. While Dr Pangloss and his ilk have the vision and technology to help you see that we live in the best of all possible worlds[11]. In Voltaire's tale, Candide learns that the world is best left to its own devices and settles to cultivate his garden.

A modest proposal: Voltaire's bestseller redux, adapted for the screen in modern form. The story of Candide was inspired by Gulliver's Travels[12], the original innocent abroad. If Gulliver were alive today, he'd be turning in his grave.

---

[11]   Voltaire, *Candide, or The Optimist* (Macmillan Collector's Library, 2020). Translation by Burton Raffel, 2006. As Candide says: 'If this is the best of all possible worlds, what are the others?'

[12]   Jonathan Swift, *Gulliver's Travels* (Benjamin Motte, London 1726).

In a twist of fate, Voltaire's library—or roughly half of it that remains intact—is kept in a special collection at the Hermitage Museum in St Petersburg. It was bought by one of his pen pals, Catherine the Great, upon his death in 1778, and transported to Russia's capital. So, about 10,000 books that fed the mind of one of the European Enlightenment's greatest thinkers are lodged in the Europe-facing former capital while the present Russian state is waging war on the West and all it stands for.

Lost sins

The Seven Deadly Sins are still real to the billions who follow a religion, however distantly. From my point of view, lower-case sins are palimpsests, lingering in generic form beneath the surface of modern mores.

Luxury is lost as a capital sin. The English word, like its French and Latin equivalents, originally meant lust or lechery. By the Elizabethan age, it had come to stand for comfort, wealth and quality. French retains the distinction in *luxe* and *luxure* (lust). Once wicked, now prized: the praises of luxury are sung in aspirational sales promotion. Lust has lost its status and ekes out a living as the sidekick of greed.

A similar shift is the makeover of sophistication, which began life as a negative attribute, now known as sophistry. Today, these are must-haves. There are glossy magazines and micro-sites devoted to luxury and sophistication and how to acquire them. People used to die of consumption, now they live for it.[13]

---

[13]   Peter Thomas Hill, *The Dictionary of Hidden Meaning*, work in progress, Zurich 2023.

Countdown

So, The Six Deadly Sins ... or maybe five. Ire—anger—is another sin of lost capitals. Who today is not irate about irritant influencers and angry at the injustice that abounds around the world? In fact, sin is now commonplace, ubiquitous, a word that stands for human weakness in all its variety. Greed is still a powerful force for evil, surviving almost intact through centuries of sophistry, sophistication and subtle shifts of meaning. Greed is good! Ye gods!

War of the worlds

However, in today's simplistic terms most things are binary. If you hate one thing, you must love the opposite—even though it's essentially the same thing. Binary confusion: the 'either/or' camp of the orthodox and obedient versus the 'neither/nor' sceptics, the freethinkers.

The two deadly sins

With that in mind, I propose that there are just two deadly sins we need concern ourselves with. The first is gullibility, the conjoined twin of manipulative lying. Gullibility is the yin to the yang of lying.

The second is unlearning: the opposite of learning. The relationship between learning and unlearning is a zero-sum game. We turn our backs on enlightenment, science and progress at our peril.

If we commit the sin of unlearning and give way to the tides of irrationality in the affairs of man, a dark and lonely world awaits: superstition, solipsism, spite and selfishness;

piracy and conspiracy; racism and fascism; sexism and all the phobias directed at fellow humans: xenophobia, homophobia, transphobia; misogyny and toxic masculinity; the lynch mob, the pillory and the gallows for those of unlike minds. The tacit seal of approval from the silent or noisy majority comes in the form of passivity or active conformism: pre-emptive obedience. These are the traits that will prevail. Liars feed on the undead minds, the ectoplasm made real, that is the credulity and malleability of the many. Knowledge is finite, ignorance knows no bounds.

The missing link

A phrase popularized in the 19th century that denoted a supposed intermediate stage in a linear chain of development from anthropoid ancestors to modern humans.

The Pre-Darwinian evolutionary theory, known as the Great Chain of Being, had many flaws. One was to suppose that evolution

Helmsman[14]

---

[14]   *Over the River*, © 2005 Quint Buchholz: http://www.quintbuchholz.de/bildarchiv/2001-2010/#bwg3/589, accessed 7 April 2023.

was linear, with fixed stages. Darwin taught us that it is a dynamic branching process. We and other primates have several common ancestors; some identified, others missing from the fossil record.

Another fatal flaw in the theory was to suppose that the chain of development is topped by a supreme being, next stage up from man. This chimed with the notion of the perfectibility of man, the endeavour of seeking oneness with the perfection of God.

Think of all the time and effort Rousseau and other great minds from Socrates onwards would have saved had they not believed in the supernatural—the least likely explanation for the mysteries of the universe.

While we linger, our lifetimes unfold in the present and perfect; once we are dead—'passed' in the current parlance—our lives are told in the past imperfect. Simplicity always breaks down into complexity, breaks up into the simpler parts of its sum. We are part of nature and therefore imperfect.[15] We grasp at whisps of meaning as they whirl without end. Amen.

The perfectibility of man

In the 20th century, the idea of man seeking perfection through reflection and approximating to the divine was replaced by the notion of enforced perfection. The Bolsheviks, declaring themselves the engineers of souls, sought to

---

[15] Leonard Cohen: 'There is a crack, a crack in everything: that's how the light gets in.' *Anthem*, The Future, 1992.

perfect *Homo sovieticus*[16]. Incurables were banished to the gulag or dispatched with a bullet to the back of the head.

Fundamentalists come in many varieties, but the species is found on every continent. Be wary of those for whom The Truth is capitalized. Absolute Truthmongers are a dangerous breed. 'I am right, and you are wrong'—seven deadly words that have wrought untold misery on humanity.

Last word on sin

The human condition: err ...

Imperfection

Fashion store window, Heidelberg, Germany, 31.10.15
© Peter Thomas Hill

How the world is conquering English: ambition and its upshot in a single word. Vaunted Hubris and vengeful Nemesis

---

[16]   Coined by Alexander Zinoviev in his novel *Homo Sovieticus*, Atlantic Monthly, 1986.

centre stage—though neither showed up at the team briefing. If only the designer and copywriter knew that their tagline was a masterpiece of hidden meaning. Precision.

A good day's work in adland: high on relevance, neatly packaged messaging, eye-catching payoff, impactful. And all the trappings just right: copy couched in web-savvy lingo, the lingua franca of global quasi-English; the fabrics eco-labelled; bang on trend for the target demographic. In short: a fist in the eye, imperfect yet sustainable, inclusive and multiversal. Perfection.

Oblivion

Consumers, young and old, stroll by. Many of the young live life in the present perfect continuous tense. The future is theirs for the taking; the past sadly passed, long buried and largely unknown, unmourned by the global now generation, assailed by influencers with pre-loved ideas and drive-by opinions, shooting from the hip—all the rage on the internet, they tell me, and that's a lot of rage. The young are now here … in the long run spelling nowhere. Oblivion awaits us all.[17]

But wait, pause for breath. Curmudgeons are archetypes as old as the human race. The Ancient Greeks bemoaned their feckless young. Socrates—bold, batty and blithe, as he was—disagreed. Despite solid arguments, he was liquidated.

Eternal verities

Let us give thanks that the eternal verities are handed down the generations, unseen but deeply felt in our learning and

---

[17]   See: *Event Horizon*, Clive James: https://www.clivejames.com/event-horizon.html.

culture, our innate kindness to one another, and our instinct for commonweal. The vital signs of the social animal in human nature are present in every newborn child. We should not be caught unawares when our shared humanity shines through the skin, thick or thin, of the young. Where there is life, there is love and hope.

The end

'This is the way the world ends, not with a bang but a whimper.'[18] But it is the Earth not the world that will end with a bang—the implosion then explosion of the dying sun. And we know the rough date of the end of days: about 5 billion years hence.[19] Just as we know roughly when we will die: sooner or later.

At 40 or 50 years of age, most of us in the cushy Western world are about halfway along the road—barring accidents, random or otherwise.

We might run into the Grim Reaper in one of the car crashes of modern life, die 'burned by the starlight of our lives laid bare'[20], or maybe succumb to plague, fire, flood, drought or a meteorite strike. Or else meet a violent death at the hands of some leader who unleashes the dogs of war: one of the Four Horsemen riding to hounds, running prey to ground, meting out injustice.

---

18   *The Hollow Men*, T.S. Eliot: https://en.wikipedia.org/wiki/The_Hollow_Men.

19   https://www.universetoday.com/152996/thisll-be-us-in-5-billion-years/, accessed 7 January 2023.

20   Quoted from *Event Horizon*, Clive James—see note 17.

© Peter Thomas Hill

But don't be fooled along the way, don't leave your path to find the foot of the rainbow. It is in your eyes and mind, not over the lake, across the field or in the woods: even if you could lay your hands on the crock of gold, it will always turn out to be a crock of shit. Greedy buggery rules. *Egosaurus rex*[21] roams the Earth ... (continues).

.

.

.

Unless ... unless ...

.

.

.

ENDS

---

[21]   Hill, *The Dictionary* ...

EPILOGUE

And in the end ... is the afterword. But no one will be left to hear it in the afterworld. And it will never be spoken. No more trees to fall unseen in silent forests. No more cats, dead and alive.

The road to Hell is paved with good intentions. The streets of Heaven are paved with gold. Hmm, this might have held true once upon a time ... but now it's surely the other way round. And there you have it. My Damascene moment, though today the road to Damascus is paved with mines.

The people of faith were right all along, but not most of them: only people of faith whose faith is in people—in others of like mind, but also in others of unlike mind, in our common humanity.

Now that we live without Sin, the world is high on poly-saturated sin—homogenized, sanitized, dietary sin. The transmigration of the soulless has taken to the air.

The human race is led by people with sharp elbows and blunt beliefs. Time for the unorthodox and freethinkers to drive out the demeaners. Time for same-size-as-life people to humble the larger-than-life go-getters. The meek shall not inherit the Earth, but the humble with the gumption to fight for what is right, to stand up for each other.

Time to accentuate the positive, eliminate the negative, and mess with Mr In-Between until we are all full of ourselves and having the time of our lives. Time for the rule of law:[22] just law, not the rule of those who are a law unto themselves. Time for Roosevelt's Four Freedoms[23]. Time and time again.

---

[22] Adis Merdzanovic and Kalypso Nicolaidis, *A Citizen's Guide to the Rule of Law. Why we need to fight for the most precious human invention of all time* (Stuttgart: ibidem Verlag, 2021).

[23] The BBC Reith Lectures 2022, *The Four Freedoms*: https://www.bbc.co.uk/programmes/b00729d9, accessed 6 January 2023.

SUPERBIA
Pride in Science and How It Can Backfire

Jabbar Moradi

> Among the real dangers to the progress of science is not
> the likelihood of its being completed, but such things as
> lack of imagination [...]; or a misplaced faith in formali-
> zation and precision [...]; or authoritarianism in one or
> another of its many forms[1].

You may wonder what the deadliest of all sins has to do with
"science" and how I might convince you that this intangible
force can have a measurable and often detrimental effect on
scientific objectivity. The pride in science could be just as
deadly as the bible considers the sin *per se*.

Merriam-Webster[2] defines pride as, first, a reasonable or
justifiable sense of one's worth or importance, second, as an
asset that brings praise or renown, and third, as an often-un-
justified feeling of being pleased with oneself or with one's
situation or achievements. The same source[3] defines science
as a body of facts, learned by study or experience. Here, I
would like to draw your attention to a few supplementary
definitions and categories, all inspired by Paul Sands' great

---

[1]   Miller, David, ed. 1985. Review of *The Growth of Scientific Knowledge*.
      In *Popper Selection*. Princeton, N.J.: Princeton University Press.
[2]   https://www.merriam-webster.com/thesaurus/pride; accessed 15th
      Dec 2022
[3]   https://www.merriam-webster.com/thesaurus/science; accessed 15th
      Dec 2022

article,[4] which is as an addition to the "pride" definition. These additional definitions will be helpful later.

Pride is different from self-esteem or self-respect, the proud are pompous and "[...] imagine themselves to be radiant with success or beauty or intelligence or virtue or piety".[5] Pride comes in three forms: vanity, conceit[6], and arrogance[7], and often, a combination of the three is manifest in the proud individual. The latter two forms are the ones I believe to be relevant for the issue at hand. Sands argues that the proud are unable to identify with others. Others are no longer seen by the proud as sovereign persons but rather as extensions of the proud one which results in that the others' legitimate needs are undermined by the desires of those blinded by pride.

I will talk about pride only in the sense of its third meaning, that is, arrogance, because I consider "science" as an achievement. An achievement that, if not for most of us who were not directly involved in the process of its production and/or proliferation at the collective level. It should be relatively easy for the reader to remember personal moments when we considered scientific results as something which we all contributed to, either financially via taxes, an indirect contribution, or by being part of the scientific community and delivering scientific research results first-hand. All personal

---

[4] P. Sands, *The deadly sin of pride*, Baylor University, School of Social Work; https://www.baylor.edu/content/services/document.php/11 7031.pdf; accessed 15 Dec 2022
[5] Ibid
[6] An exaggerated opinion of one's virtues and accomplishments.
[7] A feeling of superiority that shows itself in a lofty, overbearing manner.

involvement can justify a sense of shared achievement, especially in today's world. Today, universities are much more materialistic,[8] in the sense of the universities' financial structure and the funds they receive from the tuition fees and the governments. Money runs almost all the show.[9]

A fundamental problem with academia and the consumers of its products

To continue with the concept of pride and its connection with science, and to help visualize what I will be talking about later, let me first present a bigger picture of some problematic issues that are connected to pride in science.

We have all seen or heard variations of the so-called "science denier", a term used to label others whose argument or line of thinking/reasoning one does not agree with. Climate change denier[10] and vaccine denier[11] are amongst the most recent examples wherever a debate could have emerged; instead, these labels smothered any. One way of looking at these labels is that they are used as a tool to morally judge individuals who do not think the same about whatever the

---

[8]   *Science for Sale: The Perils, Rewards, and Delusions of Campus Capitalism* (Chicago: The Chicago University Press), 2007.

[9]   My elaborations should not be understood as an attack on science proper. My intention is to argue in general that which I consider as pride in science. This pride has animated us, Western civilization, and any community that has it as a role model to, directly or indirectly, hold scientific achievements as the ultimate source of inspiration for decision making.

[10] https://www.theguardian.com/commentisfree/2020/jul/30/climate -denier-shill-global-debate; accessed 15 Dec 2022

[11] https://chicago.suntimes.com/2021/8/18/22631335/anti-vaxx-deni ers-resisters-covid-gene-lyons; accessed 15 Dec 2022

subject of disagreement has been, regardless of how sophisticated or substantiated their arguments might be when judged by an independent referee. This matter could be analysed in many ways; here, I want to offer only an overview of why this theme matters and why we must always be aware of how the certainty of one's own morality and the desire to stay above and apart from groups of different opinion can influence our own perceptions.

A random chat with MA and PhD students, postdocs and professors suffices to realize that many, myself included when I was a PhD student, are unaware of the wealth of literature about and material on the philosophy of science. This ignorance implies the following questions: how could or should one look at science? What are the main schools of thought on how science functions and can science cause harm if it remains unchecked?[12] I am not criticizing academics who lack specific thematical understanding. We do not need to have a scientific qualification in electronic/combustive engine mechanics to safely drive a vehicle. One can be as illiterate as I am about mechanics yet drive safely, because safety is reinforced and reassured with sophisticated legal

---

[12] Not to mention the very unfortunate and extremely crucial issue of unchecked publications that some researchers take as valid and use as the basis or supplement to their research even when they are retracted, undermined, or rejected later, on https://retractionwatch.com/the-retraction-watch-leaderboard/top-10-most-highly-cited-retracted-papers/). This phenomenon should be expected in an academic set-up like ours; the pressure to publish drives scientists to cherry-pick relevant material. The list of disqualified research publications is not that short; you can find many ways of enjoying this website and discovering the depth of the issue https://retractionwatch.com/; accessed 15 Dec 2022

norms and a set of traffic rules. Naturally, in this specific case, I focus on Western culture.

What I am criticizing is that we lack a sophisticated culture and set of rules regarding science. Concerning the scientific fields that can have a direct impact on us, we do not have much of a culture or established procedures in place to hold us and scientists accountable to avoid causing (un/foreseen) harm. This fact should be even more alarming, especially since we have been told to "trust the science"—though of course, what is often meant by that is: "trust the scientists/experts that I have recommended to you"—and "do what science tells us". This lack of procedure has taken a dangerous, if not mistaken, turn in our times. A stark example was provided by the discussion about COVID-19; how it was understood[13] and dealt with. Scientific experts had been delegated to develop policies, for example concerning how, when and with how many to socialize, who would be permitted to attend a relative's death bed, whether to vaccinate during a pandemic or before it, what age groups are at risk etc. The impact of those policies on our lives—the physical and psychological effects—were still not fully understood.

As I have mentioned before, with accompanying footnotes where relevant, researchers and experts tend to cherry-pick material that supports their investigations and often their initial inclinations, sometimes even though they

---

[13]   Check here a wider range of retracted Covid research https://retracti onwatch.com/retracted-coronavirus-covid-19-papers/; accessed 15 Dec 2022

had already been retracted from the respective journals.[14] This is a serious issue for the scientific community. It becomes even more serious when we superimpose the understanding and perspective of other members of society, especially that of leading social figures, or as Thomas Sowell calls them the "self-anointed" intellectuals.[15] I have a difficult time convincing myself that the issue is not even worse when it comes to media and journalists who are end users of such research findings and even less aware of how much bias and how many unfounded assumptions could be deliberately or unconsciously injected into any scientific work prepared for presentation to the wider public.

Multiple factors influence the behaviour we have just described. To list a few: the lack of understanding that science, scientists and scientific research are not the same; the teaching in our schools that science is a progressive process built upon past scientific experience in a linear manner;[16] the level

---

[14] It is hard to overemphasize this issue; one can spend hours just scrutinizing one source: https://retractionwatch.com; accessed 15 Dec 2022

[15] Thomas Sowell, "The Pattern of the Anointed", in *The Thomas Sowell Reader* (New York: Perseus Books Group, 2011), 148-170.

[16] "Scientific education has no equivalent of the art museum or the library of classics, and the result is a sometimes-drastic distortion in the scientist's perception of his discipline's past. More than the practitioners of other creative fields, he comes to see it as leading in a straight line to the discipline's present vantage point. In short, he comes to see it as progress. No alternative is available to him while he remains in the field." Kuhn, Thomas S. 1962. Progress through Revolution. In *The Structure of Scientific Revolutions* (University of Chicago Press).

of trust assigned to the scientific researcher[17] as the embodiment of a seeker of truth; and lastly, our general ignorance of the financial factor, which has had a significant impact on many academic environments to the degree that they are often run as businesses, i.e. as money-making enterprises.[18]

Can we fit PRIDE into this picture?

I think Thomas Kuhn's diagnosis of the misleading role of the school system, the way our educational science books are written, and the unquestioning trust[19] in science in its current practice—a level of trust predicted to decline[20]—could

---

[17] Piotr Sztompka, *"Trust in Science: Robert K. Merton's Inspirations"*, 2007 https://journals.sagepub.com/doi/10.1177/1468795X07078038; accessed 15 Dec 2022

[18] Greenberg, Daniel S. 2007. *Science for Sale: The Perils, Rewards, and Delusions of Campus Capitalism* (Chicago: University of Chicago Press).

[19] The remnants of trust our predecessors had in "scientists" as seekers after truth—pure and simple—was passed on to us as a cultural heritage which we now express towards today's researchers and professors. These days, of course, most but not all are science workers rather than scientists. It is not hard nowadays to find those who are taking their academic position (a PhD or postdoc or, worse, a professorship) as a job. Job in the sense that you would not do it if you were not paid! Not to mention that the more you invest your years in research the less you are marketable for other professions and changing course becomes harder if not impossible; even if you did find yourself uninterested in science later on, you would still have to continue with it!

[20] "In our time we have witnessed the emergence of a different model of science characterized by dependence on huge financial resources, privatization and secrecy of research, commodification of research results, bureaucratization of scientific institutions and instrumentalization of science by subjecting it to extra-scientific interests. In this period of `post-academic science' ... the decay of trust in science is

explain the unrealistic and unfounded trust we have in current, post-academic science. This groundless trust in its turn inflates the existing, maybe healthy doses of pride most of us have when talking about science. This pride, often in the form of conceit and arrogance, is especially visible in the anointed intellectuals. This could explain the demand that we should submit ourselves to its dictates; to the proud person, pride in science is the only legitimate source that tells us how to behave to survive a health crisis of whatever origins.

It is clear from the unfounded trust and the conceit and arrogance that go hand in hand with it that a public figure or an ordinary person like most of us could lose touch with reality; one could also see others as extensions of oneself, demanding to silence their needs or views and have them obey the same solution found by a person who preferred the cherry-picked parts of science. It is just one further and simple step to call the "other" a denier,[21] which is often taken with no hesitation whatsoever. In recent years, we have seen and heard so many examples of this accusation online and in the media; that is the reason I do not deem it necessary to present more examples here.

The consequences of this pride-contaminated approach could easily branch out to myriad scenarios, most of which

the predictable result." Trust in Science: Robert K. Merton's Inspirations, Piotr Sztompka, 2007

[21] So much so that someone even had to define what a science denier is: https://www.urbandictionary.com/define.php?term=Science%20Denier; accessed 15 Dec 2022: "A person who openly denies results published by the global scientific community, usually for economic or political reasons." A definition that already overlooks, and is a showcase for overlooking, what I have already offered in this text.

we could list under Karl Popper's concern regarding scientific authoritarianism. Not to mention that this approach, if taken further, could mean that one specific narrative of science is accepted, funded and allowed to be followed.[22] All of which, given Popper and Kuhn's works, only means that our approximations of how things work, i.e., science, will become more and more unreliable, not to mention that our conjectures on what is true becomes a dead dogma, just like John Stuart Mill has warned us of. I have been thinking, of course, in an almost completely abstract fashion in this essay; however, the damage of a global single approach to a problem and how successful it has been for its solution, and what unseen consequences are to be discovered, is already visible in the approach we have been pressured to adopt regarding Covid.[23]

A way out of this vicious circle?

I want to remind the reader that I am not trying to offer a solution or a full and precise account of what is happening.

---

[22]   I have already shared my concerns on this matter and how high US officials were demanding the silencing of a group of scientists whose results they did not agree with in *PC on Earth: The Beginnings of the Totalitarian Mindset*, ibidem press.

[23]   This is not only a matter of freedom to try different approaches, which, given the universe we are living in and the nature of knowledge and how we are able to acquire it, necessitates such freedom, but it is also a matter of scale (I urge readers to try Nasim Nicolas Taleb's works and note his explanation of scale and its importance. When a decision is taken on a large scale and we consider the chances of its failure or success, the cost of a failure of that magnitude are too great and sometimes pose an existential threat to the society that took the decision, while the same society can often afford the cost of failure for smaller-scale decisions.

However, I found this to be a very alarming issue that we need to confront. That said, if we all agree this is one of the manifestations of the sin we should avoid, the way forward in my eyes is to have some element of caution and humility. We need a culture of humility, a virtue to cure the vice. True humility is based on realistic self-assessment which provides a balanced judgment, a judgment that enables one to recognize one's faults, achieved via introspection. It is the true antagonist to ego-saving validation.

It is only fair to acknowledge that not all scientists, public figures, and laymen have the time or interest to gain a proper understanding of the philosophy of science, although it would be very beneficial for society. I do not wish this to be taken as a condemnation of scientists'—or anyone's—lack of understanding. I have no illusions: I do not think that the solution is to educate everyone who enters this business, or anyone who consumes the products of science, in the philosophy behind it, as attractive as this may sound. A solution could be a system that declares the evolutionary-based philosophy of science to be the rule of the game, allowing mutations and natural selection to run their course. A system that does not provide an authoritative and specific view of science but enables only what benefits the development of science and knowledge in the long run. A set of rules that prevents governments from letting their agendas influence the research directions they are funding, a trend that currently incentivizes researchers to formulate grants to the satisfaction of grant committees. We need a solution that allows all relevant ideas to have a platform for securing funding and offers an opportunity to challenge others.

AVARITIA

Tight-Fistedness Concealed behind Pseudo-Ethical Statements

Josette Baer

San Francisco, CA, USA, November 2019

My friend and I are sharing a room at the convention centre, a large hotel downtown, member of an international hotel chain. We are attending the annual conference of our academic field.

A couple of days into our stay, I enter our room to change; I spot, upon opening the door, a small green flyer on the floor. It says on the first page, showing the picture of a middle-aged woman with South American looks holding a shield:

> "Refuse the hotel's green choice program. Green choice hurts us!"[1]

The reverse side of the flyer reads:

> "The hotel's green choice program isn't that green [...] Zero leading environmental studies recommend skipping housekeeping. Climate leaders are already rejecting the program [...] Housekeepers report using more water and chemicals to clean filthy rooms. It is another kind of green: Hotel owners boast to investors about how much

---

[1]   Flyer, page 1.

money they've saved. [...] It cuts our hours and incomes. In just 6 hotels in 1 year, housekeepers lost an estimated 1.7 million dollars in wages and benefits. It makes our work harder. Housekeepers report increased workloads, inquiries, and pain due to the program. Refuse the hotel's green program during your stay and demand the hotel create a sustainability program that addresses climate change."[2]

If these statements of the housekeepers' interest group are true, and why would I doubt their truthfulness, then this "green program" is an outrageous sin of avarice, a moral crime against the weakest members of US society—the working poor who lack education. How desperate must these women, often immigrants, be to secretly distribute cheaply photocopied flyers during their daily shifts, cleaning our rooms and bathrooms, asking the hotel guests to support them? Can they not talk to the management, the CFO and CEO? Notice, that the flyer does not mention a worker's union.

I am speculating now: this flyer activity is the cleaning ladies' last resort. If I cannot talk to my employer, fearing that I'll lose my job the minute I am making demands or protesting, I must find a different solution. Socialism and Communism were movements born of desperation, exploitation, and poverty. Marx and Engels' analysis of Capitalist exploitation was a fresh and modern view of the world, but they were mistaken in psychological and logical terms: not every entrepreneur or factory owner exploits his workers just because

---

[2]   Flyer, page 2.

he is wealthy and wants to make more money. Capitalism per se is not to blame, just ruthless and greedy Capitalist employers. The logical fallacy of Marx and Engels was to interpret Capitalism, the system of paid labour and free markets, as the principal cause of exploitation, as causation, not correlation. Only if workers owned the means of production, would they be free from capitalist exploitation. If I am a greedy and heartless factory owner, exploiting my workers is not causally connected to my budgeting, it is, from my greedy point of view, an additional bonus or, cynically speaking, collateral damage. My greed is thus in a correlative relation to my Capitalist entrepreneurship, that is, my entrepreneurship does not automatically make me a greedy person.

If I am a decent entrepreneur, I take care of my labour force, because I know that people who are well fed, receive healthcare, and earn a fair salary, deliver better work in terms of quality. Marx and Engel's logical fallacy, so fervently promoted by Lenin, Stalin, and the Soviet leaders, Gorbachev included, led eventually to the collapse of the Soviet satellite states in 1989 and the Empire's centre, the Soviet Union, in 1991.

Human beings strive for physical and financial safety, and for that, they are eager to work. Safety for what? To bring up the offspring, to procreate, to have a family. This is evolutionary biology. As clever and educated as we might be, or think that we are, we cannot escape our nature; the evolution of our species *Homo sapiens* is based on procreation. Nature does not care if we like this basic principle or not, and nature is not fair. Our species' aim, or natural drive, is survival by adaptation to a changing environment.

A chain so wealthy that it has hotels all over the globe masks its avarice, its naked greed, by professing a pseudo-ethical commitment to the environment, with no regard or consideration whatsoever for the people who keep the hotels running and make customers come back.

I like nature, clean water, fresh snow, the sun and the stars, flowers and trees, and animals. Who does not? But would I not rather first help a human being from starving to death? In my humble opinion, the "green program" is nothing other than shameful virtue-signalling at the cost of the working poor who have no voice against the hotel's managers. In the last fifteen years, I have stayed at several hotels belonging to that same chain, and the rooms were always impeccably clean. Why? Because the cleaning ladies did an excellent job.

One just has to look at the intimidated faces of the housekeepers, trying to smile happily, when they knock on your door, asking permission to come in and clean. I have always felt sorry for them and left a tip I could afford. The shy and grateful smiles on their exhausted faces told me all I needed to know about their employment situation. What made me sad, once I realized the financial brutality of their lives, was how grateful they were to receive a tip of some five British pounds or some ten US dollars from a woman who was younger, who could have been their granddaughter.

I know nothing about the wages of the housekeepers at that hotel, or the hotel chain's salary policy, which might vary from state to state, according to the market situation. Yet, one does not have to be an economist, HR manager or housewife to understand the cynicism of the "green program": a simple experiment suffices.

Let us suppose that for the limited period of a week, a different friend stays every night at my flat. Because I want to save water and cleaning products, I decide to clean the bathroom after friend no. 7 has left at the end of the week. By now, what do you expect the bathroom to look like? It is a cesspit of bacteria, dirt, in short, a very unhygienic place. To clean it, I would probably have to spend at least three hours, if not longer. It is rather obvious that I would save water, cleaning products and time if I were to clean the bathroom every day on a five-minute schedule. This daily regime would also be advantageous for my body, my physical wellbeing. Everybody who has scrubbed a bathroom for ten minutes experiences severe pain in the back, arms, and neck.

Reverend Stalker, elaborating on the deadly sin of avarice, does not say that being wealthy is a deadly sin, but the love of money is the sin.[3] As would, say, deciding to keep my money instead of helping another human being, all the more so as I can afford it. Greed, tight-fistedness, and avarice are thus mindsets that are sinful.

I am not a religious person, but I adhere to the principles of Christian ethics, because they make sense to me. How can a society take care of the poor if there are no wealthy people? The deadly sin of avarice leads thus to a situation where those who can afford it, refuse to help those in need. If everybody is equally poor, who owns what? That would be the state and its unelected administrative personnel.

---

[3]   Stalker, 22.

Economy and science, whether we like it or not, are the principal activities that promote the survival and progress of mankind. Without funds, labs and universities we cannot engage in research and develop medication such as vaccines. Without funds, talent cannot be promoted through education, and international organizations cannot take care of the poor in the Third World. Money is needed to develop eco-friendly cars, sustainable sources of energy, and new eco-friendly textiles made from recycled materials. Money is a means that puts food on our tables. At first glance, money can buy me friends, or rather persons who allegedly like me for who I am. Once my money is gone, just watch who will still be around! Money can thus buy loyalty, but that loyalty is limited by time and money. True and honest loyalty does not care about money, as illustrated by the Godfather movies. The Corleone clan's criminal activities are successful because the clan members are bound to each other by family ties. Money allows me freedom of mobility, decision-making and security. It allows me to have excellent healthcare when I am old, frail, and ill. Yet, money cannot buy me happiness.

Reverend Stalker suggests three principles of fighting avarice as a mindset or consciousness. *First*: "There are better things than money; good health is better; a sympathetic heart is better; a clear conscience is better." [4] *Second*: "Money is not an end, but only a means to an end." *Third*: "Money cannot be kept forever." As simple or simplistic as these principles may sound in theory, they prove wise when we apply them to daily life. First, if I am chronically ill and

---

[4]   Stalker, 34-40.

wealthy, I can afford superb healthcare, but would I not rather enjoy good health? Second, if I regard my wealth as an end, I forsake the good I can use it for, to use it as a means to achieve a more important goal than to have it accumulating at the bank: I can help charities, found schools, universities, vocational training, thus goals that help the younger generations to have a better life.

A touching example of the second principle was the Czech entrepreneur Tomáš Baťa, who built an entire factory village in Zlín.[5] His shoe company is a global success story. Baťa, born into a working-class family, had an immense talent for business and investment, and a firm belief in "entrepreneurship with a human face".[6] Finally, principle three: why can I not keep my money forever? Because I will die, and if I die wealthy, my children and grandchildren will be very happy. Whether they keep the wealth they have inherited from me, or gamble and speculate it away, is beyond my influence. The best I can do to prevent that is to educate them.

To conclude: avarice is a deadly sin. The hotel's "green program" is hypocrisy *par excellence*; it is a perfect example of virtue-signalling, of pretending to do something for the planet, which is a petty trick to increase shareholder value by heartless and cruel exploitation of the housekeepers. Such practices are also short-sighted; the hotel chain has lost me

---

[5]   The Baťa company built factories, vocational schools, housing, recreational institutions: https://www.visitczechrepublic.com/en-US/82a3fe9b-e0fa-44ca-b40c-c93a1a0c1ee0/place/t-zlin; accessed 10 January 2023.

[6]   I have coined this slogan or description for this essay. It is an interhistorical slogan, referring to Alexander Dubček's Socialism with a human face.

as a customer for good. So shall any company or chain in the private market economy that behaves avariciously, masking its greed as eco-friendly, diversity-aware or gender-conscious at the cost of the employees. More on gender equality, the feminist concept of justice and mob mentality in my essay about ENVY.

INVIDIA
Toxic Feminism[1]—or When a Man is the Victim

Josette Baer

> "Rape is an outrage that cannot be tolerated in civilized
> society. Yet feminism, which has waged a crusade for
> rape to be taken more seriously, has put young women
> in danger by hiding the truth about sex from them. [...]
> Leaving sex to the feminists is like letting your dog va-
> cate at the taxidermist's."[2]

In recent years, the West has experienced social movements,
interest groups, and factions engaging in activities on behalf
of principles they understand as the new pillars of social justice.[3] These new pressure groups or activist groups distinguish themselves from the older interest groups such as the
gay and LBTQ movements, which have been making a difference for their members since the 1960s and 1990s, respec-
tively.

---

[1] https://www.quora.com/What-do-you-think-of-the-term-toxic-femi
nism.; accessed 12 January 2023. Toxic feminism is a concept that still
requires definition; one could speak of a pluralism of opinion. Therefore, I will present my own definition.

[2] Camille Paglia, "Rape and Modern Sex War", in *Free Women, Free Men.
Sex. Gender. Feminism* (New York: Pantheon, 2017), 52-57, 52, 53.

[3] An analysis of social justice activism and its theoretical basis can be
found in my "The Salemization of the US Campus? A Liberal Critique
of Identity Politics (IP)", *COMENIUS Journal of Euro-American Civilization 8*, no. 1 (2021): 89-107.

BLM[4] went violent. In the summer of 2020, in the aftermath of George Floyd's death, BLM activists occupied Seattle's Capitol Hill, the cultural centre of Seattle with restaurants, bistros, theatres, music halls and dance clubs. The activists declared it an autonomous zone. The police moved out. Seattle mayor Jenny Durkan of the Democratic Party, who on US Sky News had referred to the CHAZ (Capitol Hill Autonomous Zone) as a sign of the "summer of love", likening it to Woodstock in 1969, which had been a pacifist anti-Vietnam War youth movement, did not condemn the violence of the BLM rioters. She probably thought that by currying favour with the mob and letting it roam about Capitol Hill she would gain political clout. Yet, what Mayor Durkan did not understand is that you can control the mob only by force of the police or military. If the mob tells the city government what to do, or what not to do, the state's sovereignty is under threat, and with that, the lives of the citizens. Instead of being grateful to Mayor Durkan for ignoring the laws of Washington State and the authority of the police— oh, the illusion!—the mob showed up at Mayor Durkan's house a few days later, threatening her physical safety and demanding she push through some BLM claims.[5]

The feminist movements Me Too [6] and Time's Up[7] were peaceful, and at the time of their emerging, there was indeed a need for women to engage against sexual abuse. The trial of Harvey Weinstein was a great success for women in the

---

4   https://blacklivesmatter.com; accessed 11 January 2023.
5   https://youtu.be/iWZYnUubUTc; accessed 30 March 2021.
6   https://metoomvmt.org; accessed 11 January 2023.
7   https://timesupnow.org; accessed 11 January 2023.

entertainment industry; the verdict demonstrated that no-body is above the law, not even the most powerful man in Hollywood. These feminist movements certainly encouraged many to speak up, revealing male abuse of power, sexual harassment and in a few cases, rape, yet the problem with both groups was the lack of definition: a covetous male stare or gaze was considered as much a violent act as rape. As activist initiatives, however, both movements deserve gratitude and respect; such initiatives have always been of benefit to an open society.

A negative aspect of recent US feminist activism, as I have come to understand it, is the *a priori* hostility and hatred of men just because they happen to be born as men. While the second wave[8] of US feminism (1968 to the 1980s) targeted discrimination in the workforce and the public space, empowering women to look after themselves in professional and financial terms, the third wave of feminism[9] (1990s) regarded men as women's enemies, *a priori*. Feminist ideology of the third wave declares that the sexes are equal in biological and psychological terms, albeit a look at evolutionary biology proves the opposite. Camille Paglia, a feminist thinker, a declared lesbian—at a time when it was dangerous and illegal to admit one's sexual preference openly—and 1968 activist knows what she is talking about:

---

[8]   https://www.gale.com/primary-sources/womens-studies/collection s/second-wave-feminism; accessed 12 January 2023.

[9]   https://www.womenshistory.org/exhibits/feminism-third-wave; accessed 12 January 2023.

"Feminism keeps saying the sexes are the same. It keeps telling women they can do anything, go anywhere, say anything, wear anything. No, they can't. Women will always be in sexual danger. [...] A woman going to a fraternity party is walking into Testosterone Flats, full of prickly cacti and blazing guns. She should arrive with girlfriends and leave with them. A girl who lets herself get drunk at a fraternity party is a fool. A girl who goes upstairs alone with a brother at a fraternity party is an idiot. Feminists call this 'blaming the victim'. I call it common sense."[10]

In Europe, feminism is understood differently than in the USA; liberal Western Europe adheres to the principles of tolerance and personal responsibility, while Eastern European and former Communist societies have a more equal understanding of the sexes because everybody earned more or less the same salary under the Socialist regime. The Communist governments also gained wide support among women, at least in the early years, because they liberated women from the three Cs: Church, Cooking and Children. Every woman had a job and earned her own money, yet women were still burdened with family work.

Before I elaborate on a man as a victim, let me present my definition of toxic feminism, inspired by the *feminist Realism* of Camille Paglia:

"Toxic feminism considers women the superior sex and believes that if women ruled, the world would be a better, more peaceful place. It ignores the biological

---

[10]   Paglia, 53, 54.

difference between the sexes and declares that every woman should be believed, regardless of evidence. Toxic feminism puts women above the law, and, at the same time considers women always as victims, regardless of evidence. Toxic feminism denies different opinion; that's why it is totalitarian. It does not acknowledge open and fair debate. It perpetuates a contemptuous view of men as the perennial perpetrators, brutal rapists by nature, and contemptuous misogynists, also by nature. It divides society instead of uniting men and women. It is toxic in the sense that it poisons human relationships, educational goals, and government policies by focusing solely on women's role in society. Toxic feminism has prompted a crisis of masculinity in the USA. The grandfathers of toxic feminism are Stalin and Hitler."[11]

Now, a man as a victim: the world was glued to the TV and news channels on the web when the trial of Johnny Depp and Amber Heard[12] began in the spring of 2022. I followed it every day. Once the news that Depp had allegedly physically abused his wife had broken a few years ago, I began to look at whatever evidence I could get online. Back then, I did not believe the accusations, for one simple psychological reason: none of Depp's former partners had accused him of domestic violence, among them Kate Moss, Winona Ryder, and

---

[11]   Have a look at Warren Farrel and John Gray, *The Boy Crisis. Why our Boys are struggling and what we can do about it* (Dallas, TX: BenBella Books, 2018).

[12]   A summary on https://www.nbcnews.com/pop-culture/pop-culture-news/johnny-depp-amber-heard-defamation-trial-summary-timeline-rcna26136; accessed 13 January 2023.

Vanessa Paradis, all of them accomplished talented actresses and models who have earnt their success with hard work. I thought it highly unlikely that Depp, all of a sudden, had changed his behaviour towards women, starting to beat up Heard at the age of fifty.

I felt sorry for Depp's children and began to boycott a leading French cosmetics company that had hired Heard as a beauty ambassador, without checking evidence. That company just believed Heard, because she was a woman and a celebrity, a status she had achieved not by talent or professional accomplishment, but by marriage solely. Before Depp married Heard, nobody knew who she was. Much like a Californian Z-list actress who married into a European royal family, Heard openly reiterated her support for female empowerment, presenting herself as a victim of toxic masculinity. The fact that she got a leading role in *Aquaman*[13] only because of Depp's influence in the industry was revealed in the Virginia court's hearings. Thus, two women, completely devoid of talent and professional acumen achieved celebrity status and money by marriage only—indeed, great feminists!

After some months of research, it was clear to me that Heard was the abuser, and Depp the victim. I am a nobody, not trained in psychology or medicine, and thus had to rely on common sense. I just went online, and the information I gathered was accessible to everybody. Various YouTube channels-conducted thorough analysis, basically confirming Heard's guilt; she was the abuser, not Depp. While a court in

---

[13]   https://www.imdb.com/title/tt1477834/; accessed 19 January 2023.

London declared Depp guilty, the court in Virginia, USA, was more diligent.

Not only the fact that Heard is a rather unaccomplished actress, the physical evidence, no wounds, and psychological analysis by Depp's team made sense. Heard was also caught lying about money she allegedly had pledged to a children's hospital. To pledge is not the same as to pay. A pledge is a promise, nothing else. I can promise anything, but when will I pay up, fulfilling my promise? Heard did not pay up; she kept Depp's money and went partying with her friends. A self-declared daughter of a working-class family, Heard came into money by marrying Depp; she certainly enjoyed her new wealth.

After roughly two months of trial, the jury declared Johnny Depp not guilty of rape, domestic abuse, and violence against his former wife. Heard was sentenced to pay Depp millions of dollars for his loss of revenue, since film companies had one-sidedly cancelled contracts with him, again, without waiting for a court's decision. Johnny Depp was not only the victim of continuous physical and psychological abuse from Heard, but he had also lost his reputation as an actor, because of the virtue-signalling entertainment companies who did not care about evidence.

The saying "innocent until proven guilty", a pillar of the Western legal tradition, did not apply to Johnny Depp. Nobody defended him; everybody in the bling-bling Hollywood sphere took sides with Heard—because she was a woman

One cannot even begin to understand the mindsets of those persons who, against court evidence, still support Heard, defending her after the verdict. The Open Letter claims that Depp fans engage in vitriolic comments on social media, harassing Heard.[14] Well, social media are media that exist because of people expressing their opinion. Toxic Feminism is full of envy—envy of whom? Reverend Stalker on envy: "Not infrequently, envy is the fruit of idleness and laziness."[15]

Let me conclude: the anger against men in general, expressed by toxic feminists, originates, I think, in personal issues that are based on a general and encompassing feeling of envy. Successful women do not need to bash men, because they are used to dealing with men in professional and private life. Those who work hard, acknowledge the hard work of others, because they know what it takes to make it to the top, to create one's wealth. Successful women like Michelle Obama, Amal Clooney, Taylor Swift, Mary Beard, and Camille Paglia have achieved their professional success through hard work, not by relying on men.

I therefore think that histrionic toxic feminists sense deep down that they are losers, losing out to success and money, and that is the reason why they are so envious: they covet fame, global attention and money, but they know they can never achieve this on their own. They not only admire women such as Heard, but also support them frantically, in an almost cult-like, brainwashed fashion. The anger and envy of toxic feminism is a convenient mask:

---

[14] https://www.washingtonpost.com/nation/2022/11/18/amber-heard-open-letter-support/; accessed 15 January 2023.
[15] Stalker, 77.

"[…] is the circumstance that while some confess that they hate a good many people, there is no one that they will say they envy […] cloaking and concealing their envy with whatever other name occurs to them for their passion, implying that among the disorders of the soul it is alone unmentionable.[16]

The self-appointed moral apostles cannot admit that they are envious of Heard, so they defend her with false sympathy and histrionic applauding.

Furthermore, the saying "believe every woman" is hypocritical and unfair to the core; it signals that only women speak the truth. This kind of virtue-signalling is not helpful, because it disrupts the fabric of society, promotes prejudice, fosters ignorance of the law and lastly, supports the ideological view that women are the better sex. Most dangerous, I think, is that this poisonous envy masked as rightful female empowerment teaches young girls and women that they, because they are female, are entitled to everything they want, without the work, discipline, acumen, and talent required. In this regard, their envy is a deadly sin, deadly to an open, tolerant society that respects the rule of law. Innocent until found guilty regardless of sex—that should be the motto of true feminists in any court case and also in life.

---

[16] Plutarch, *Moralia, vol. VII* (Harvard: Harvard University Press, 1959), 97.

GULA
Gluttony

Katarzyna Suboticki

Obesity is the cultural epidemic of our time. Whether you look at the USA, Great Britain, Mexico or Brazil, or even Asian countries, the percentage of seriously overweight and obese adults—and, tragically, also children—is growing each year all around the world. Simultaneously, we have ready access to a broad range of information on nutrition and health-related issues. No one can be in any doubt that obesity is, to put it mildly, unhealthy. Among the consequences are heart disease, type-2 diabetes and cancer. A body weighing 400 or 500 pounds cannot function well with all that weight to carry—the body functions *despite* it. To state this fact today is to attract scrutiny from many social media micro-movements. We have all encountered them one way or another. Combined, they fall under the self-proclaimed, female-led "Fat Acceptance Movement". The movement has been around for decades, but it has recently gone into overdrive and reached mind-blowing intensity. Its incentive? Superficially (and in many cases certainly genuinely) it is to sensitize society to the often cruel treatment of overweight women. However, the oft-repeated goal is to convince the world that health and attractiveness *can* go hand in hand with extreme weight. To claim otherwise is discriminatory, derogatory, sexist, downright uneducated. It is an evolution of the "Body Positivity Movement", which largely went and still goes against unrealistic und dangerous beauty standards in the media. (Some keywords: Facetune, filters, and Photoshop used in magazines and on social media.) "Body positivity" (in itself a very positive term) has now been largely absorbed by the group that coined terms like "fat-phobia in medicine", according to which physicians who claim that obesity is harmful to physical and hence mental health have succumbed to societal pressure in cruelly promoting one body type: the slender, fit one. How did it come to this? Of course, the media's impact on brain development in the younger generation during a formative phase of their lives is as crucial as the culture that feeds off it.

But looking back, you have to start somewhere in the search for a leitmotif running through all this. Let's try here:

Who remembers the late nineties? Those of us who were around to experience the rise of blonde teenage pop princesses who would dominate the charts, news and (horrible) fashion for years will remember that it was also a time of change in media coverage of those young women: Christina Aguilera, Jessica Simpson, Mandy More and their ilk. And of course, the queen to rule them all—Britney Spears. Frenzied media attention, with meticulous analysis of her every step, outfit, performance and body change was the daily norm that eventually led to her breakdown. It was unprecedented. Press obsession reached new heights when it came to the polite, rather shy girl next door from Mississippi. As did fan veneration. (Recently proven with the "Free Britney" movement that ended the singer's guardianship.) It goes without saying that such a level of loyalty and admiration inspired emulation in every sphere of life for many years to come. Apart from the blond mane, her soft silky voice, catchy songs and sweet, bubbly personality, her distinguishing feature was the cropped tank-top—with low-cut trousers, of course. Brittney's belly button virtually defined that era. As did Britney. Before the all-encompassing internet and social media, she was the unquestioned superstar and her influence on teenagers around the world unmatched. It is not possible for anyone who wasn't Britney's age or younger at the time of her explosion onto the music scene in 1998 to get their heads around the impact she had on generations of teenagers' fashion, the perception of their bodies and sexual representation. Legions of girls swore to remain chaste until marriage because Britney did. Her body was obsessed over day in day out. Did she gain weight, did she have a boob job, does she take the pill to make them grow? Her healthy figure—petite, toned but not starved—was considered the new perfection and stood in stark contrast to the unattainable Heroin Chic of the nineties, epitomized by the waiflike Kate Moss. Britney's Lolita-look and sexy dancing was risqué and shocking for that time (not by today's standard in any shape or form) but fascinating, and in retrospect it laid the groundwork for today's over-sexualized representation of women in music.

Whatever it was, Britney tapped into a cultural niche that made her a mega figure for emulation. She was second only to "The King of Pop" Michael Jackson. The press had a field day.

When her stardom was in decline in the mid-2000s, media obsession and the vacuum of personality cult had to fix on a new idol to entertain the masses. Eventually it was Kim Kardashian who filled the void and in her own right changed the world—as tragic as it may sound. With the full force of social media, a knack for business and an understanding of the glamour of narcissism she became a billion-dollar entrepreneur and single-handedly changed the perception of what is considered "sexy" about women's bodies and their presentation. It didn't happen overnight. At first not taken seriously, with the help of her now ex-husband Kanye West she was transformed into a fashion icon and plastic sex symbol. A surgically enhanced caricature of the female form became the new "go-to" for millions of young women. "Bigger" became acceptable. But it wasn't without the footnotes. It didn't involve a healthy layer of fat—it applied to the oversexualized form that came with butt implants. Usually paired with fake breasts, fish lips and Botox injections in your twenties. Logically, it didn't have much to do with natural attainability—a wasp waist does not naturally go with bulging butts and huge breasts. But it nevertheless shifted the cultural norm of perceived female attractiveness. The new female look consisting of extreme derrières became desirable and enriched the cosmetic surgery industry with a new cash flow. Kim made exaggeration and fakeness socially acceptable. Was it around that time that the unnatural started to move into the mainstream as the new norm? It is not unlikely.

The growing trend towards excess, along with exposure through social media, brought all kinds of movements into the public eye, closely followed by groups that could exploit that interest. Add to it the continuous sugar-coating of facts in favour of protecting feelings at universities all around the USA and you have the perfect fertile soil for mass outrage over criticized delusions.

You're healthy whatever your size as long as you love yourself—this could be the mantra for the fat acceptance movement. You can overindulge in the unhealthiest foods, not be able to find your waist as a result, but as long as you respect your choices and love who you are, you can even be an ideal role model for your child, for young girls on the internet and wider society. And no one should even dare suggest that other choices might be beneficial to you. Obese models like Tess Holiday criticize the fact that their exposure in the media is considered controversial. This is not quite correct. It is not the body that is controversial—but it is controversial to claim that it is healthy just because you happen to be spared from the long-term ill effects of your food choices.

Food choices and their visual effects on the body and lifestyle have always been in motion and reached different shores. Food was and is prestige and religion. In both extremes.

Being unnaturally skinny is still—in certain circles—an admirable statement of strong will opposing the temptation of attainability of food in excess. Restraint in the face of abundance. I am thinking of the nouveau riche from China and Russia and the untouched, overfilled plates of food left behind in hotel rooms and buffets. The Oscars adorn the menus for their multimillionaire guests with edible layers of gold while the latter preach sustainability and humility from their podiums.

A prominent group are the skinny vegan pseudo-environmentalists, who treat their body as "a temple" to be nourished with organic "environmentally friendly" superfoods from China (toxic goji berries), Mexico and Peru (mafia-supervised avocados) and Spain (water-draining almonds). To such people, an organic carrot is the solution to all world problems (and a materialized rendition of their unique personality). They of course chronicle every enlightened choice they make as they fly around the world to experience exotic places with untouched nature.

History buffs will know how the ancient Romans, before the fall of their perverted decadence, dealt with excess in terms of food during their orgiastic feasts. The less history-oriented remember it from the popular novels and movies of the "Hunger Games" series where the blasé citizens of the Capitol (the centre of the totalitarian dystopia) would do the same—eat until they could eat no more and then use potions to regurgitate the food so they could continue to engage in their gluttony, all the while a large portion of the population was on the brink of starvation. Gluttony wasn't suitable for the masses, of course, but reserved for the high-end members of society.

Today, Mukbang videos across the internet frame the food frenzy in inviting surroundings on YouTube and are watched by tens of millions of young viewers. Food is clickbait for followers; health is secondary.

If you make it as an oversized or obese person in the music industry, you unknowingly (by now probably very knowingly) sign a silent contract with a part of your fan base that showers you with love and support, not only because of your talent, but also because of the representative power of your body shape.

American singer and rapper Lizzo is also a self-declared icon of the body positivity movement. She has repeatedly called out anyone warning of the dangers of her obesity as haters and declared her body to be art. She is also aware of her footing with her fans who admire her self-confidence, which she demonstrates on a regular basis in skimpy bikinis or with nothing on at all. When in 2020 the news got out that Lizzo went on a short detox, the outrage among her followers was enormous. Was she, after all, a traitor to the body positivity movement? Was her self-confidence feigned? Not at all. Lizzo felt the responsibility to clarify that she was in no way attempting to lose weight but had gone for a detox to give her body a rest. The world of Lizzo's fans was in balance again.

This can't be said of many fans of Adele after the singer actually dared to lose over 100 pounds over the course of two years and presented her new body to the world with a single picture on Instagram in 2019. The outcry went through the roof. Even Adele, who never capitalized on her obesity to gain fans, was met with scrutiny and disappointment. She was indeed a liar and traitor to the inclusivity community that had embraced her as she was, fat and all. The woman who rose to superstardom despite being obese and claimed to be body positive had dared to wake up and change her life for the better. People were shaken, as their "safe space"—Adele's Instagram and Twitter accounts—got infiltrated by the health police that made their idol go against the body positivity community. Adele, however, didn't entertain the obsession over her new weight and quickly put a lid on it two years later with a simple statement with no further comments. She rejected any responsibility for others when it came to their body image. Case closed.

You can spin the madness further. Nowadays being "anti-fat" (whatever that means) can also be considered racist. Why? Because so-called fatphobia ostracizes mainly fat women who happen to be black. Due to structural discrimination, black female Americans often have a much harder time resisting obesity. And with the bias against their bodies, the health issues often stem more from the accompanying mental problems than the actual obesity. "This heightened concern about their weight is not new; it reflects the racist stigmatization of Black women's bodies. (...) Today, the idea that weight is the main problem dogging Black women builds on these historically racist ideas and ignores how interrelated social factors impact Black women's health. It also perpetuates a misinformed and damaging message about weight and health." (Stings and Bacon, 2020) Yes, healthy food is more difficult to get in many minority communities, where fast food chains have spread to graciously accommodate the low-income households with their fair share of food made affordable. Yes, it is more expensive to eat healthily in the USA than to live off grease-fried burgers and fries. Yes, black communities battle bad schools and poor education. And yes, poverty is linked to obesity (and that goes for all communities). But to conclude from all these points that it is innate hatred of Black female bodies that drives the concerns is another level of ignorance. The contention is that it cannot possibly be the exploding health costs, nor the immobility and unemployment that eventually awaits all the morbidly obese—it is racism.

The food industry is also fighting health hard. Manufacturers take great advantage of our evolutionary biological weakness to crave fat and calories (just in case a mammoth shows up around the corner and we have to run for our lives). Naturally, they come up with all kinds of versions to stimulate our fat receptors and make us come back for more. Any limits or regulations on the selling and purchasing of any kind of addictive food (i.e. containing large amounts of processed sugar, ideally with trans fats) is, after all, to the detriment of those food chains.

Aggressive advertising aimed at children, including eye-level displays at grocery stores, cute forms of bottles perfectly fitting a child's little hand plus the mandatory brain-addictive amounts of sugars are all around and have led to an epidemic of obesity from the youngest age. Small steps are being taken. New York City managed to ban sodas as the default drink in kids' menus. They can still be bought separately. A more useful proposal of banning the use of food stamps to buy sodas was rejected by federal agents (McGeehan, 2011). It wasn't possible to distinguish what falls under the definition of sodas, obviously.

It is important to remember that many children in the USA think of canned tomatoes or frozen beans as fresh food. That their chicken leg on the table grew in a lab unattached to a chicken because they have never seen one. That eggs are formless because they only see them as liquid in huge plastic tubes with dozens of egg whites inside. You would laugh if you didn't have to cry. So, disregarding whether you're a fan of the Obamas and Barack's presidency, under the consideration of where the USA stands when it comes to education about nutrition, Michelle's attempted contribution to the health of the nation's children during her husband's two terms in the White House has to be worthy of the utmost respect. But alas, this intrusion went against many parents' (and companies') perception of their freedom—the rock the United States is built upon, after all. Hence, any advice, let alone demand, that elementary schools ban greasy fries and canned sweetened milk as the only options on their lunch menus in favour of fresh salads and baked potatoes was, understandably, a direct threat of socialism sneaking in to catch the youngest of the nation. It is hardly surprising that these kids will grow up being proud of their free choice of having become obese on their own terms.

The scorn with which Michelle Obama's gardening of fresh vegetables with kids was met in the conservative media was in itself ridiculous and devoid of any logic. It just proved once again that the media (on both sides) are more concerned with partisanship than the actual well-being of their citizens if it means giving props to the other political side.

For a while, the inclusivity changes were admirable and way overdue. Representation in television, literature, entertainment and merchandizing; Black and Asian barbies were introduced after the decades of tall, blonde, white ideal figures; heavier Barbies than the anorexic original; dolls with amputated legs, in wheelchairs; dolls with skin burns. Body positivity didn't celebrate obesity, it went against the equally dangerous starved runway model look and the propagated tips from that industry to eat cotton balls soaked in orange juice to give the body the illusion of food. It opened the door for acceptance of different natural body types, issues like lipedema, vitiligo, skin problems. The message: nobody is perfect; perfection is an unhealthy illusion. No sane person would ever claim that appearance doesn't matter.

A certain difficulty in fighting this absurd, destructive movement presents itself in the blending of two conflicting areas: the justified fight against truly discriminatory language and behaviour on the one hand, and the crazy demand for negation of facts and admiration for anything someone feels (allegedly) comfortable with on the other. As an example, the term "summer body" is often considered toxic (Dall'Asen, 2022). It comes with connotations of course. Fitness, flat stomach—the industry makes billions every spring convincing women that they need to get the newest stuff to get into shape. "Get beach ready" means get fit and usually, also get thinner. But wouldn't anyone choose a healthy fit body if it was available with the snap of the fingers? It is the effort that is dreaded. The long years of giving in to uncurbed appetite aren't easily erased with a crash diet. Admitting to a certain level of food addiction and personal weaknesses takes courage and some painful tough talking with oneself. Banning the term "summer body" isn't going to make you feel healthier and better about your obesity. It's listening to experts who respectfully point out solutions to your evident problem and try to push you towards a healthier path (no doctor is going to demand that you have toned thighs).

After all, if Pinterest blocks the term "thinspiration" from its search engine because it encourages anorexic and bulimic (mostly) girls to seek out terrifying pictures of starved bodies and "inspirational" sayings like "Hungry to bed, hungry to rise, makes a girl a smaller size" to keep them going why is it that morbid obesity is being celebrated as body acceptance nowadays? Nobody is suggesting mobbing heavily over-weight or obese people, nobody demands they be banned from flying (except Katie Hopkins) or lose their jobs or that they shouldn't be able to find a swimsuit that fits and be harassed at the beach. A logical question, however, is to ask why they are supposed to be celebrated for their obesity. And not helped. Respected but encouraged to get healthier and hence prolong their lives? This taps deeply into identity politics—in which the idea, the perception of truth, is inextricably linked to the person owning or uttering it. Hence, if I am an obese person and you don't accept (whatever that may mean, it goes in the direction of admiration) my size and my subjective perception of my body, you're not just disagreeing with me on that issue (obesity is unhealthy)—you are attacking me as an individual, my dignity as well as my worth in society and with your mindset you are directly contributing to an oppressive climate that makes my everyday life miserable. After all, I'm allowed to speak "MY" truth. If you question it, you are denying me the space in society to exist safely without being reminded that I'm slowly killing myself.

Of course, just like every injustice in our modern Western society, fatphobia is also a direct consequence of the poisonous oppressive patriarchal structure that has forced women into sexually desirable frames of thinness, logically, for men's own gratification. It is no coincidence that the fat acceptance movement rose from feminist circles that see men as the source of every evil in the world. Heavily overweight women losing weight is considered a toxic pattern enforced by patriarchal society that women submit themselves to in exchange for admiration. They fell into the honey trap. The fat acceptance movement knows better.

Bibliography

Dall'Asen, Nicola, "Will the phrase 'summer body' just die already? Here's how we can end the toxic saying for good". June 16, 2020. https://www.glamourmagazine.co.uk/article/power-of-plus-summer-body

McGeehan, Patrick, U.S. Rejects Mayor's Plan to Ban Use of Food Stamps to Buy Soda. August 29, 2011. https://www.nytimes.com/2011/08/20/nyregion/ban-on-using-food-stamps-to-buy-soda-rejected-by-usda.html

Spring, Sabrina; Bacon Lindo. "The Racist Roots of Fighting Obesity". June 4, 2020. https://www.scientificamerican.com/article/the-racist-roots-of-fighting-obesity2/#

Center for Science in the Public Interest. March 28, 2019. https://www.cspinet.org/news/healthy-kids%E2%80%99-meal-movement-grows-passage-new-york-city-bill-20190328-0

IRA

Finis Idealism—Back to Political Realism?

Josette Baer

"The criticism of idealist illusion is not only pragmatic, it is also moral. Idealistic diplomacy slips too often into fanaticism; it divides states into good and evil, into peace-loving and bellicose. [...] The idealist, believing he has broken with power politics, exaggerates its crimes. [...] States engaged in incessant competition whose stake is their existence, do not all behave in the same manner, at all times, but they are not divided, once and for all, into good and evil. It is rare, that all the wrongs are committed by one side, that one camp is faultless. The first duty—political, but also moral—is to see international relations for what they are, so that each state, legitimately preoccupied with its own interests, will not be entirely blind to the interests of others."[1]

When French political theorist Raymond Aron (1905–1983) published his theory of international relations in Paris in 1959, the world was divided into two ideological camps: the free West and the totalitarian Soviet bloc. That ideological divide was referred to as the Cold War (1948–1991) because both camps had nuclear weapons with the potential to wipe out humanity. This was a very dangerous situation,

---

[1] Raymond Aron, *Peace and War. A Theory of International Relations* (London, New York: Routledge, 2017), 584-585, italics by me. Aron's title is of course an intertextual reference to Leo Tolstoy's great novel War and Peace.

unprecedented in the history of mankind. Governments and leaders who did not want to commit themselves to either camp chose to join the ideologically neutral movement of non-aligned states, established in 1961 by Yugoslav president Josip Broz Tito (1892–1980).[2]

In December 1991, the Soviet Union dissolved, and the free West declared that it had won the Cold War (1948–1991), which, I think, was an accurate assessment back then, because all satellite states in Eastern Europe chose, by democratic vote of the people, to establish a new democratic regime and a market economy, thus going West: Poland, Czechoslovakia, which separated peacefully in 1993, forming the Czech and the Slovak Republic, Romania, Bulgaria, and Hungary. Yugoslavia was the only state that fell apart by means of a cruel civil war, which ended in 1995 with the Dayton Agreement; the former Yugoslav republics Slovenia, Croatia, Serbia, Montenegro, Bosnia-Herzegovina, and Macedonia became independent states. Most of the former Communist states had achieved EU and NATO membership by 2020.

East Germany was reunited with West Germany thanks to Mikhail S. Gorbachev's (1931–2022)[3] generosity and his need for funds to bring back the Soviet troops stationed in the satellite states. Back then, Western leaders promised in the 2 plus 4 talks that if the Soviet Union allowed the reunification of the German people within the borders drawn by the victorious allies of WWII, NATO would not go one step further

---

[2]   The best biography of Tito known to me is Jože Pirjevec, *TITO. Die Biographie* (München: Verlag Antje Kunstmann, 2016).

[3]   An excellent biography is William Taubman, *Gorbachev. His Life and Times* (London: Simon & Schuster, 2017).

towards the east; this was a confirmation that Russia would not have to feel threatened by the new power constellation in Europe, with reunified Germany as a NATO member. With hindsight, this was a very bad deal for the Soviets, because they gave up their *cordon sanitaire* for a promise.

The Western leaders promised by lip service, no signed contract—mind you. In those years, the Russian government was weak, the country burdened with economic problems. Some individuals, most of them former members of the Communist Party in their country and in the right position at the right time became very rich very quickly. Western companies poured into the former Communist countries and went on a shopping spree, buying up state-owned companies and factories.[4] This was referred to as privatization, thus economic regime change, but it was *de facto* corruption. Corrupt government officials sold off the people's assets for a bribe. The wild goldrush years of the 1990s affected Russia most cruelly. A goldrush is characterized by the absence of law, the rule of the jungle; in the 1990s, the goldrush in the East was of a financial nature, and Russian governmental rule too weak to stop it.

The subsequent attempts of the West to influence and dominate what became the Russian Federation in 1991 also prompted the US view of superiority in terms of political theory: democracy and the free market had won and proved that the end of history, in Hegel's understanding, had been

---

4   Kazimierz Z. Poznanski, "Building Capitalism with Communist Tools: Eastern Europe's Defective Transition", *East European Politics and Societies 15* no. 2 (2001): 320-355.

achieved in political and economic terms. Therefore, following Francis Fukuyama's (*1952) interpretation of Hegel (1770–1831) the world should understand that the West's political, social, and economic organization was superior, the ultimate and best political organisation mankind could ever achieve. Maximum freedom for the citizens was what Hegel, inspired by the French Revolution of 1789, had promoted, but he had not been specific, because of the censorship that could have put him in prison. Democracy, the rule of law state and market economy were, in Fukuyama's thinking, the end of history.

Why? Because human self-organization could never achieve a more human, just, and free form of government. The end of history means the end of the struggle for the best constitutional arrangement, the most benevolent constitution for the citizens, granting them freedom of speech and association, a blind *justitia*, and the right to leave your country if you don't like it. It also allows the right to run for office, government administration and top military positions that, prior to 1918 in Europe, had been the privilege of the aristocracy. Therefore, the end of history does not mean that mankind ceases to exist, but that it shall be prosperous, democratic and happy, what the American constitution refers to as the pursuit of happiness.[5] Political freedom is liberty, and the East Europeans knew very well what that meant, having experienced the rule of the state secret service, the closed borders, the planned economy that enslaved individuals and the

---

[5]   The US constitution on https://www.archives.gov/founding-docs/constitution-transcript; accessed 26 January 2023.

idea that entrepreneurship is exploitation, and ownership is theft.

As a student of political theory and East European history in the early 1990s, I had embraced Fukuyama's idealistic and, based on the political events back then, also realistic analysis. Today, in 2023, I have changed my views, because the global situation has changed. In the 1990s, Idealism ruled, an almost euphoric embrace of democracy and the free market economy, ignoring how citizens in post-communist countries, especially Russia, struggled. Indeed, if you had grown up in a state that took care of your education and career, providing free healthcare, life-long employment, and a pension you could survive on, the collapse of the state institutions painfully affected not only you, but also your family.

Now, in 2023, we should think about political realism, choose rational thinking, and look at the world as it is, not as we would like it to be. First and foremost, the Russian Federation is a new state, in no way comparable to the Soviet Union. Since 2014, the West has poured sanctions on to Russia for her annexation of Crimea. To the West, the annexation was a violation of Ukraine's sovereignty, while Russia acted out of strategic thinking: if Ukraine joined NATO, the port of Sevastopol would not only be lost to the Russian Federation but present a serious military threat at Russia's door. A political equivalent would be Russia or China occupying Cuba or Canada, which would threaten US sovereignty. Who lost China? Who lost Russia? The USA, I think, are in dire need of a diplomat of the calibre of George F. Kennan (1904–2005).

Justified and explained with the slogan of American exceptionalism, the USA considers herself as the global leader,

holding the self-declared right to dictate international relations and how states should organize their social and economic order. Just establish your legal, political, and economic
systems like ours, or at least be our faithful ally, and then you
shall be fine—or so US political leaders, congressmen and the
White House must have been thinking since December 1991.
After all, we beat our principal enemy, the Soviet Union, the
Evil Empire, as US President Ronald Reagan (1911–2004)
once said. Considering the strong US economy, they are right,
or so I, a Swiss liberal, thought just some years ago.

In terms of democracy, the rule of law, civil liberties and
the sovereignty of the people, the USA are certainly the leading nation in the world. Americans, as I have come to know
them, having lived in Seattle for three years, are most generous, welcoming, and friendly towards foreigners and immigrants, because they understand themselves proudly as a
melting pot[6] of humanity on their continent, the embodiment of the Enlightenment ideas of equality and freedom.
Melting pot means: nobody is a stranger, we are all human
beings, from whatever culture you descend, you are welcome in the USA, the land of the free. You are a human being,
and the first amendment of the US Constitution grants free
speech as a fundamental right.

Yet, if the American people understand themselves as
the beacon of democracy and the most rightful nation in
moral terms, what are the origins of the USA's sense of

---

[6]   On citizenship and the US melting pot see the superb Victor Davis
Hanson, *The Dying Citizen. How Progressive Elites, Tribalism and
Globalization are destroying the Idea of America* (New York: Basic
Books, 2021).

mission, which deems it appropriate to lecture other countries with widely differing cultures? Is this sense of mission really based on a general feeling of love for mankind, the wish to liberate the oppressed and the mission that every nation in the world should adopt the political system the USA has so successfully established since the American patriots chased out the aristocratic British in the revolution of 1776?

In Aron's thought, political realism does not equal Machiavellianism, thus the practice of lying and cheating appears benevolent, and rather have the citizens fear the ruler than like him. Since the Florentine statesman's thinking about political rule was expressed in the 16th century, domestic politics and international relations have significantly changed. When Machiavelli wrote his *Prince*,[7] he wanted first and foremost to avoid civil war born from the weakness of a ruler; his advice to Lorenzo di Piero de' Medici, also referred to as Lorenzo il Magnifico (1449–1492), was to stay in power at all costs. Losing power would throw the Tuscan principality into the abyss of civil war, with domestic factions fighting each other, prompting invasion by their respective allies—and with that, cause the people immense suffering. Therefore, political realism in the 21st century does not mean to lie, cheat, and oppress your citizens, on the contrary: accountability, responsibility and trust are key words of political realism, especially in international relations.

---

[7]   Niccolò Machiavelli, *Il Principe. I Discorsi. Con introduzione e note di Adolfo Oxilia* (Sancasciano Val di Pesa (Firenze) 1935 (8), first edition 1926.

Under what conditions can I trust my enemy? I can trust my enemy only if he and I agree on a contract that binds the two of us together, limiting our hostile escalation of political and military activities. Treaties and contracts worked well in the Cold War: treaties were negotiated, and the USA and the Soviet Union respected them. A treaty is, in political theory and practice, the most ethical instrument of sovereign governmental rule and relations with a hostile state. Why? Because a treaty is based on my free will, rational deliberation, and willingness to compromise. A treaty is based on minimal consent, that we both play by the same rules; it is a political instrument that is based on procedural morality, as all parties have the same weight, the same power. I sign a treaty only if I agree with its stipulations. If I am truly sovereign, nobody can force me to sign a treaty, if I don't like its stipulations; I keep negotiating and so does any other party, until we all agree on the conditions favourable for us signing the treaty and then, the stipulations of the treaty.

What are the conditions of compromise? I am willing to compromise only when I, with rational deliberation, understand that a peace treaty is a better option than the risk of going to war. War is always a risk; it should be avoided, but sometimes, a war has to be fought, especially if the aggressor has an unhinged mind, like a certain Austrian *Gefreiter* in 1939 who believed that a cultural and religious minority in the European diaspora was responsible for Germany's defeat in WWI. The Munich Agreement concluded in October 1938 was the West caving in to the *Gefreiter's* threat: give him the Sudetenland, and we shall have peace in Europe. This appeasement, masked and presented as international compromise, did not work, and Czechoslovakia, the only democracy in Central Europe in the interwar years, was sacrificed for a peace that did not last even one year. On 1 September 1939, Nazi Germany invaded Poland.

Therefore, the contract theories are indeed a good school for anybody interested in political realism: Hobbes, Locke, Rousseau to a certain extent, and Rawls, while Kant's *Perennial Peace* is a masterpiece of rational and enlightened thinking. The international treaty is the art of compromise.

Now, why adopt political realism in our times? Why bring back the political thought of the Cold War? Because it worked. Unlike idealism, realism is a mindset and behaviour that is free from ideological entrapment; it means to look at the world the way it is, not how I would like it to be. Realism means being willing to work together, to avoid war, to protect one's citizens. I can conclude trade deals with anyone as long as I keep to that which I have signed. To conclude a treaty is a rational activity, born of clear thinking, the knowledge of my actual power and strength as a state and the knowledge of what I want from the other. As a rational agent, I can conclude treaties even with those states whose culture, political regime, and faith I truly hate, because signing a treaty is a rational act, my feelings do not play a role. Only from a position of realism can I de-escalate international conflicts or prevent them from emerging.

Just think about the Thirty Years' War in Europe (1618–1648): Catholics and Protestants fought each other for thirty years, and their factions brought immense suffering and misery to the Europeans. Counties, towns, and villages had to change faith according to the confession of the marauding occupying troops, sent by various duchies and states. Friedrich Schiller's (1759–1805) *Wallenstein*[8] is a superb poetic description: the Moravian warlord was victorious and wealthy, and lastly betrayed by his Catholic allies, because he had become too influential, meaning that he could have ended the war for the Catholic faction. Paradoxically, he was disturbing the balance of power between the Catholics and Protestants that was required to keep the war going on.

The leaders of both confessional camps stopped only when they understood that no party could win, when Europe was devastated. Why could no party win? Because it was a confessional war, both camps fighting for the right faith. I cannot convince you of the superiority of my Protestant confession, and neither can you convince me that I save my soul by converting to Catholicism, because there is no supra-confessional final decider who tells us who is right. God kept silent in Europe in those cruel years.

An equivalent of the Thirty Years' War was the Cold War, because it involved two political systems that were diametrically opposed: the Communist view of the world understood itself as the liberator of the oppressed workers; once Socialism would rule the world, Capitalist exploitation would be a thing of the past. The West promoted liberty, democracy, and free markets.

What will the future of international relations look like? At the time of writing, in September 2023, the BRIC states are

---

8   The dramatic poem in original German on https://www.projekt-gut enberg.org/schiller/wallens1/wallenst.html; accessed 4 February 2023.

enjoying great popularity in parts of the world one used to refer to as the second or third world. For our political future, which is the future of our children, I would like to suggest the realism of Raymond Aron, because only matter-of-factness, respect and accountability can save mankind, regardless of the various political opinions, cultural differences and diverging beliefs that exist on our planet.

ACCIDIA
Idleness—The Default Strategy in the Age of Indifference and Indecisiveness

Pavle Krsmanović

The Sloth

Sloths are charming, tree-dwelling mammals inhabiting the tropical forests of Latin America[1]. Their most notable characteristics, by which they earned their name, are their inertness and general slowness of movement. In fact, the characteristic passivity of these animals is thought to be part of their evolutionary strategy: their largely nocturnal life and slowness of movement allow them to avoid being noticed by many of their potential predators.

Another connotation of the word *sloth* is the human characteristic of unwillingness to work and overall laziness. Unlike the animals, who are seen as charming and characterised by carefree idleness and enjoyment of slow-paced life, people described as *sloths* are generally viewed in a less positive light. In particular, *sloth* is one of the seven capital sins of Christianity, where it denotes carelessness with regard to others and particularly indifference to the supposed duties to God[2].

If one looks beyond the medieval religious connotations of the sin, its most appropriate modern analogue could

---

[1] Gardner, Sloth, *Encyclopaedia Britannica*.
[2] Delany, *The Catholic Encyclopedia*.

simply be a form of indifference to society in general, apathy regarding broader social matters, or even the ways one's acts might, perhaps even inadvertently, affect others. Since humans have evolved cognitive capacities which allow them to comprehend the world they live in and decide how to act, *sloth* in their case could be denoted as of a *cognitive kind*: as someone who does not bother weighing their decisions in a consistent, coherent or merely conscientious manner. Therefore, whereas in the case of animals the idea of *sloth* emphasises indolence as a beneficial evolutionary strategy, in humans as social animals it is associated with what one might call *cognitive*, rather than *physical inertness*.

One might further assume that *cognitive inertness*, as a means of blending into the social background and not questioning the dominant social norms, could be a valid approach to strengthen one's social belonging and thereby similarly qualify as a successful strategy for flourishing in the context of human societies. However, a responsible citizen in modern times is commonly thought of as one who is willing to be involved in broader social matters, some of which might ultimately, but not immediately, be of one's own personal concern, and ideally make decisions in line with the moral framework of the modern society one is a part of. Although the problem of people's lack of broader communal engagement may have been around throughout history, the increasing and overwhelming interconnectedness of people all over the planet nowadays makes the question of such engagement more pertinent than ever. Yet, the sad truth seems to be that the more connected we are globally the more distant from each other we have become.

The increasing interconnectedness of people has created an enormous flow of information, which is glorified as one of the ultimate virtues of modern times. It allows us to make our own decisions freely, unconstrained by any interfering factors. Yet, the associated endemic problem of having such a flood of information available is that some pieces of it often conflict with others, thereby making the original ideal of free choice more difficult to fulfil. The problem seems to be that people's prevailing indifference to broader social considerations stems from the fact that we are ill-equipped to deal with such a vast amount of information which may be biased, incorrect, or even deliberately misleading. One might easily be misled into believing the decisions are autonomous, i.e. one's own, ignoring the danger of being unknowingly manipulated or emotionally swayed into making a decision not in accordance with one's own interests or even going against the interests of society.

In order to revisit the respective problem, particularly in a more modern context, I start from the idea that one's unwillingness to engage in critical thinking, let alone in debating with an open mind about many of the current issues, stems from the fact that one is overwhelmed with conflicting information regarding what decisions to make and how to act. I argue that, given such circumstances, one's innate *sloth* might make a default, easier and more straightforward choice, thereby compromising one's own integrity. I look into the approaches at one's disposal to make informed decisions and to decide who, or which pieces of information, to trust. I further cite an example of a recent and still ongoing matter of conflicting information about vaccination and argue that such situations lead to what one might call a general social or cognitive inertness, idleness and, ultimately, apathy. After discussing the problem in the context of cultural and sociological developments in modern times I briefly reflect on what might be done to escape it.

Justifying beliefs

One commonly associates personal beliefs with a set of opinions reflecting one's world view, those which one holds without necessarily questioning them but rather having adopted them as part of one's own persona. Any position on matters of fact is a form of personal belief, something that we are fully entitled to have. The liberal wisdom of the modern day holds that we are all entitled to our own, personal beliefs, regardless of how (un)true or perhaps even ridiculous they might be. Therefore, one's view that the Earth is flat is, semantically at least, as much of a belief as that it is an oblate spheroid which is slightly wider at the equator than at the poles, and that it spins on its axis. One would easily spot that these two positions are mutually exclusive, and only one of those beliefs could be held at any particular time. As it happens, the latter of these two beliefs appears to be true, or for the sake of fair debate and open-mindedness we could say that it is true at least as far as one can possibly know, whereas the former one is false. As we are all entitled to our own beliefs, and many of us are entitled to express those beliefs in public, it is not surprising that some of those false beliefs are held by a significant number of people.

The question remains as to what means one has at one's disposal to judge which of those beliefs have higher merit and could thus qualify as knowledge. The debate on what are the necessary and sufficient conditions to consider as knowledge any *belief* that is *true* has a very long and interesting history. One of the earliest traces of it in Western philosophy can be found in Plato's dialogue *Meno*. In the dialogue Socrates has with Meno it is revealed that what makes knowledge superior to mere *true belief* is the justification that one has for holding it[3]. As is often the case in philosophy, the issue has been debated ever since, particularly since the 1960s[4].

Despite being aware that we do not possess evidence for every single supposedly *true belief* we hold, and thereby think that we know it, the majority of us are still quite confident that most of what we consider knowing is true and that we are somehow justified in believing it. At times some of those pieces of knowledge are so well engraved on our minds that we have come to think of them as highly intuitive, as if they had been there with us from very early in life. Hence it would seem that, at times, one would feel confident claiming to know things which happen to be true and which one

---

[3]   Plato, *Meno*.

[4]   The question of knowledge and the relevance of its valid or justified sources have appeared in many different forms throughout history. The theme peaked in the 1960s, when Edmund Gettier (1963) described examples of cases which show how one could formulate beliefs that are true yet that happen to be justified only by sheer luck. According to him, such cases would not quite qualify as knowledge, as one commonly thinks; the original definition of knowledge representing justified, true beliefs would need to be supplemented with a qualified statement on the impact and relevance of luck. Although not everybody agreed with the conclusions of Gettier's thought experiments, they did shape the debate that emerged later.

believes in, despite not having any substantial, objective justification, apart from one's own partial recollection or even
intuition, following one's faculty of reason.

Even though Immanuel Kant, one of the major proponents of the rationalist school of thought during the Enlightenment, was a fervent supporter of primacy of reason, he has
acknowledged a key insight on the importance of empirical
evidence from the empiricist camp, that of David Hume.
Namely, in his attempts to dismiss the idea of metaphysics,
the realm beyond the material world, Hume pointed out that
all our insights, our innate views and intuitions that seem to
come from *reason* alone, are in fact *borrowed from experience*[5]. Furthermore, Hume held that any *a priori* deduced
connection between causes and effects is impossible and
that it is only the information gained through our experience,
via our senses, that provides us with the necessary evidence
for the particular pieces of knowledge. Kant extended Hume's
view to claim that such evidence would further serve to gen-
erate understanding of the physical world[6], thereby justifying
our claims of knowledge.

Nevertheless, it is clear that not all our knowledge is justified from the evidence that we have collected ourselves,
particularly in this day and age. Thus, as in the case of our
planet being an oblate sphere, most of us—excluding astro-
nauts who have travelled beyond our atmosphere and seen
the Earth from distant orbits, or perhaps sailors who have
voyaged around the world—would have no direct, personal

---

[5]   Kant, *Critique of Pure Reason*, 49.
[6]   Kant, *Critique of Pure Reason*, 172, 256.

evidence that the Earth is not flat. Nowadays, we tend to trust reliable sources of such information, or the data they have generated which supports it, such as visual evidence about the shape of our planet in the form of photographs generated from outer space.

At first sight, one who could be deemed a (human) *sloth* might appear to simply be cautious and rather critical, though not fully sceptical, about some novel piece of information, but merely not allowing oneself to jump to conclusions. In general, one would think that holding any position already widely accepted among one's peers might in fact be fully rational, as is the case with widely accepted *true beliefs* such as those regarding the shape of the Earth. One deemed a *sloth* might simply seem to be more prone to following the trends of a particular (sub)culture more stringently and even unconditionally, having segregated oneself and being surrounded by echo chambers. Since members of any such group would have a number of commonly shared beliefs, the group would act as a buffer between them, a means of establishing and promoting trust among its members.

The desire to be affiliated to a group of any kind seems to be innately human, as is perhaps the case with many primates. Since beliefs held by different groups could often come into conflict with each other, the defenders of a particular set of beliefs, being segregated to a specific group, might build a strictly partisan attitude to the beliefs in question in order to express firm loyalty to the group they belong to. Thereby, perhaps ironically, belonging to these close-knit groups prevents one from coming closer to many others on a more direct, human level, unless they happen to belong to the group one already shares some beliefs with, ultimately leading to a decline of one's sense of universal empathy and community.

Establishing trust

The greatest problem with respect to forming new beliefs we all have is deciding whom to trust, particularly in cases when we are facing contrasting claims about a matter on which we wish to decide but that we are only superficially familiar with. In order to make decisions in cases of conflicting stances, one judges the justifications for the claims that one is considering. Such justifications could come either in the form of evidence or, in most situations for the vast majority of people, from the supposedly reliable sources of the information in question.

Many, if not most of us might like to think of ourselves as independent, free-thinking, autonomous individuals who weigh the pros and cons of any given choice, perhaps not necessarily overly thoughtfully or pedantically but sufficiently so not to seem too credulous. It is nevertheless clear that most of the information we collect is not easily verifiable by ourselves alone, whereby we need to decide which sources to trust. Therefore, the traditional norms of reliability or experience of something as being a means to secure justifications nowadays are not sufficient. In order to secure sufficient justifications for regarding some of our own and others' beliefs justifiable we tend to weigh the reliability of sources of information and the trust we have in them as the proxies to weigh the justifications.

Ever since the Enlightenment, and particularly since the industrial revolution, we have witnessed significant improvements in the living conditions of more and more people. Part of the improvement is due to the fact that society has become richer, and the distribution of wealth has improved, despite the occasional notable setbacks in the process of establishing more egalitarian societies. Yet another, perhaps more significant, factor that played a role in this progress was the numerous scientific discoveries and associated engineering developments. We have thereby come to rely more and more on science in a wide range of fields, including transport, communication, industrial development and medicine.

Since in the case of most of these scientific applications, all the achievement was meant to be somehow external to ourselves, we have overwhelmingly greeted it. Yet in the case of medicine some still seem more reserved. Perhaps the unease many feel with regard to certain medical improvements is that these are perceived to be more intimate, as they interfere with our physical self. Interestingly, most improvements in technologies met with wide approval, yet once the spotlight fell on the issue of sharing personal information and tracking many became more concerned and reserved about the matter. In the case of medicine, one of the clearest examples of a similar distinction could be regarding differentiation between taking some medications orally to fight the disease or receiving injections for it, or vaccines to prevent it, whereby many people might find the former somewhat less invasive, and hence preferable, compared to the latter options.

The difficulty with following the guidelines of modern medicine is exacerbated by the fact that a lot of it relies on scientific research, conducted in specialised facilities far from the eyes of the public. Therefore, when it comes to medical treatments the general public is expected to trust findings from scientific data, which is understandable to a minority of people and in some cases accessible to very few. Bearing this in mind, it is perhaps not surprising that a substantial proportion of people still harbour reservations, if not outright scepticism, about many biomedical scientific findings, or anything else they are less familiar with. Furthermore, considering the restricted availability of its data, biomedical science might be perceived as elitist and wilfully difficult to comprehend. Yet, since the general public is expected to make rational and informed decisions about such issues, the question of their relevant skills naturally comes into focus. Since most people are not professionally skilled in matters of biomedicine, one could say that their capacity to make rational and informed decisions independently in those particular cases might be compromised.

Bearing in mind the previous point about scientific work remaining very distant from and unclear to the general public, it is not surprising that the question of trust has gained prominence. Yet, the reliability of scientific methods and approaches to gain insights and obtain knowledge about natural phenomena has been worrying scholars for centuries. The question of how meaningful and broadly applicable scientific findings are has been thought about intensively ever since Hume posited that our past experiences, as would be the case with even reproducible scientific investigations, are not a logically valid basis for assuming that the same will happen in the future[7]—the problem that troubled Kant as indicated above.

Some two centuries later, Karl Popper offered a different view of the problem, trying to give what one might call an empirically pragmatic response to Hume's concerns. Namely, instead of focusing on scientific enterprise as the process of proving that certain natural phenomena are universal, which Hume concluded not to be possible empirically, he suggested that its focus is in fact on trying to disprove such claims. In other words, he refocused the worry about the belief in scientific knowledge by claiming that we cannot trust the scientific theories entirely, since we have no strictly logical reason to expect that the future will entirely reflect the past; yet we have good reason to trust them, until proved otherwise[8]. Thereby, Popper introduced the concept of falsification, the idea that the true goal of science is in fact in trying to disprove its own theories. As radical and paradoxical as this position might seem at first sight, it enabled science to be confident about its

---

[7]   For a more concise version of the argument, see David Hume, An Enquiry Concerning Human Understanding, Section 4. Hume acknowledged that we tend to make inferences about the way we expect the future to be from the experience of similar events in the past, but also stressed that we cannot make definite causal connections between any two events a priori. In other words, even though one might think that some events are plausibly connected, one cannot assume a necessary connection between them. We cannot assume that the events we have seen will resemble future events, because there is no logical justification that would be universally valid. The reasoning associated with this idea is the so-called problem of induction.

[8]   Popper, The Logic of Scientific Discovery, 10, 17-20, 32, 33.

endeavours, even though its inferences could never be empirically tested, in every possible scenario—such as in other galaxies. Instead, scientific claims would be made after being sufficiently and rigorously tested, thereby making them extremely likely to be true, and remain valid until counteracted by some other, previously unknown evidence. A further significant aspect of Popper's thesis was that it clearly demarcated the space between science and pseudoscience, the latter being an endeavour issuing claims which allege to be factual and scientific in character but in fact remain based on suspect claims derived by non-scientific methodology. In Popper's terms, such claims would remain at least in part untestable and, more importantly, entirely unfalsifiable[9]. In order to avoid any possible misunderstanding, what ought to be clarified here is what is meant by the pseudoscientific claims being unfalsifiable. In order for any claim, be it true or false, to be falsifiable there has to be a method which, if the claim in question were false, would demonstrate that. For example, the claims coming from the long-standing practice of predicting one's future or character based on positions and movements of celestial bodies, known by the name of *astrology*, cannot be falsified as the predictions are never concrete and precise enough. The fact that it might appear to yield correct predictions in some instances could be a matter of luck or merely a result of vague and unspecific claims which would allow for a vast number of interpretations, some of which would allegedly support the predictions. Furthermore, we have no approach to discern how exactly these celestial events impact an

---

[9]   Popper, *The Logic of Scientific Discovery*, 13-15.

individual's persona or future and thereby make any testable, verifiable claims. To avoid sounding overly patronising, it could be pointed out that we have not discredited astrology as a practice of some sort, perhaps as a type of light-hearted entertainment, as it is everyone's personal right to believe in it; we have merely shown that it is just not scientific in any way, even if it (mis)uses scientific language to legitimise its pseudoscientific ideas in a seemingly credible manner.

Unhealthy scepticism

Most of the above discussion about medicine implicitly deems it a personal matter for each person. Although that might be the case in many, perhaps the vast majority of such issues, since one's own health is primarily one's own concern, there are cases where individual decisions could have far-reaching, broader societal consequences. One such case is the matter of infectious diseases and particularly vaccination as a means of preventing their spread. Although the idea of variolation as a means to combat smallpox is over 200 years old, with the practice of immunisation using remnants of old, infected material as a means of building up immunity against it being widespread practice in China and India for hundreds of years before that[10], the idea of mass vaccinations worldwide has gained prominence only in the latter half of the twentieth century. It is hence perhaps not surprising that vaccines are perceived as a fairly modern phenomenon, particularly with the rise in prominence of multinational pharmaceutical companies, whose primary motives might not be seen as

---

[10]   Boylston, *The origins of inoculation*.

humanitarian. Interestingly enough, although one might think that an unwillingness to get vaccinated is due to lack of information, it is worth pointing out that of three countries which ranked highest for distrust in a survey of confidence in vaccines, two, France and Japan, are members of G7[11]. In general, the countries with a higher mean of years of education are more likely to report greater mistrust of vaccination; yet, within those countries higher education correlated with more positive views on vaccine effectiveness and importance, but not safety. Although in some of these countries, such as in France, the mistrust of vaccines arose in part due to previous controversies concerning hepatitis B and HPV vaccines, the widespread resistance to vaccination in rich countries shows that lack of information and insufficiently broad education of people are unlikely to be the main reasons for scepticism against vaccines in general. In fact, a byproduct of the availability of information is also the availability of misinformation, particularly of a pseudoscientific type, which might foster further controversies.

The reason the issue of vaccination has become so important is that it is not solely a matter of personal choice if one should get vaccinated or not, but also of responsibility towards the community. Ironically, due to their effectiveness, vaccines have become *victims of their own success*, as the diseases they are designed to prevent have become less familiar to the general public, many of whom then see fewer reasons to participate in vaccination programmes[12]. Hence,

---

[11]   Larson et al. 2016.
[12]   Yaqub et al. 2014.

perhaps expectedly, the most common reasons for vaccine hesitancy are lack of awareness, low perceived severity of illness and belief in alternative medicine. On the other hand, the reasons for healthcare professionals' hesitancy towards vaccination are concerns over vaccine safety, such as being dangerous for pregnancy or promotion of allergies.

The case of importance of vaccination is even more pertinent bearing in mind that individual decisions could have more dramatic consequences for others, by allowing easier spread of the virus the vaccines are designed to target and thereby permitting it to mutate further, eventually making the existing vaccines less effective. The mistrust of vaccination in the ongoing Covid-19 pandemic has by now surpassed the question of justifiable concerns regarding severe side effects in a small minority of cases and become a distrust in the science altogether[13].

The widespread rejection of vaccination is even more surprising considering that, of those who object, often only a small minority is firmly against vaccination, whereas a large majority is merely indecisive. In fact, vaccine hesitancy is thought to arise due to doubts about the benefits of the vaccines, doubts about their safety and questioning the need for them, all of which would eventually lead to refusal in those cases[14]. As the indecisive majority is being bombarded by

---

[13]   European Medicines Agency (EMA) press release on AstraZeneca's Covid-19 vaccine. One should of course acknowledge that there are some legitimate fears concerning the safety of some vaccines. Therefore, vaccine efficiency and safety concerns should be addressed more honestly and transparently, particularly in the respective case of one of the Covid-19 vaccines.

[14]   Yaqub et al. 2014, Larson et al. 2016.

conflicting ideas and instructions, many coming from populist politicians or even alleged experts, it is perhaps surprising that hesitancy is not higher. Bearing the sources of such conflicting information in mind, it is worth pointing out that medical resources, family and friends) were favoured as sources of information by proponents of vaccinations, opponents generally favoured the media[15].

Scepticism vs open-mindedness

Having an open mind for diverse opinions about a matter of public interest tends to be seen as a positive trait, since insisting firmly on any particular position in such matters could easily make one seem uncompromising and difficult to discuss any matters with. Yet, the belief that one is likely to be more objective by considering many possible theories could be misguided, since some of those theories could simply have no factual basis. The attitude of uncontrolled plurality of ideas is fertile ground for pseudoscientific claims, not necessarily because of the lack of any sound, factual knowledge but more likely due to the full egalitarianism of the supposed authorities behind the claims, at least in the public's perception of their reliability.

One example of what one might call a pseudoscientific theory in the ongoing Covid-19 pandemic is that 5G network technology is responsible for the outbreak and propagation of Covid-19. The variants of this theory seem to take two different forms: either that 5G itself, rather than an allegedly nonexistent SARS-CoV-2 virus, causes the disease or that the

---

[15]   Czajka et al. 2020.

5G network somehow weakens the immune system thereby allowing the disease to spread more easily. The first one of these claims could be responded to by simply looking at the publicly available data of the number of times the virus has been isolated and sequenced. Namely, since November 2019 when the virus was first identified, over 360,000 peer-reviewed scientific manuscripts on the work related to Covid-19, or over 200,000 referring to SARS-CoV-2 have been published[16]. Furthermore, the complete virus has been isolated and sequenced over 1,380,000 times since its first isolation in January 2020, thereby identifying a number of new variants and confirming the existence of the virus over and over again[17].

---

[16] The latest numbers can be easily verified by accessing publications databases, such as the PubMed Central of The National Center for Biotechnology Information, which is part of the United States National Library of Medicine (https://pubmed.ncbi.nlm.nih.gov/)). Search for publications about Covid-19 or SARS-CoV-2, beginning November 2019.

[17] To access the records of the complete and publicly fully annotated available sequencing data of SARS-CoV-19, one can use the Covid-19 section of the source presented in footnote 17: (www.ncbi.nlm.nih.gov/sars-cov-2/) and access the Nucleotide records. To see how many of those are from the complete genome, one can click on the Nucleotide Completeness menu heading on the left side and choose the complete reads option. The number of complete records can be found next to the option in the drop-down menu, but one can also inspect each of them individually. Another platform sharing data on viral epidemics is GISAID: (//www.gisaid.org/); it presents assembled epidemiological and clinical data associated with Covid-19 of more than 14,400,000 virus sequences. The number of publications and sequencing reports of the virus is growing at a very high rate; the figures cited in the text are from 30.12.2022. 15 months earlier, on 16.09.2021, there were over 181,000 and 122,000 published manuscripts that had Covid-19 and SARS-CoV-2 as keywords. More than

The second claim about the 5G network affecting the immune system is easily debunked if one simply compares the countries with the high Covid-19 outbreaks, which includes India,[18] and those where 5G networks are already available, which does not include it[19]. Finally, an ongoing comprehensive study on the question of 5G impact on health indicates that the 5G network could only lead to minuscule and negligible local rises in temperature around machines using it, nothing that could lead to an outbreak on the scale of the Covid-19 pandemic, although to make any fully founded claims further studies are clearly needed[20].

Coming back to Popper's idea about falsifiability and verifiability of scientific claims, one could clearly see why these 5G network theories have no place in any scientific discussions, since in those cases scepticism about a virus causing Covid-19 is supplemented by a conspiratorial belief that it is the 5G network that is causing the disease, based on completely unsubstantiated claims and often supposedly privileged information which therefore cannot be verified. Even if there were a higher correlation between the installation of 5G networks in different countries and the outbreaks of Covid-19, that alone would not mean the two would be causally correlated. Further pseudoscientific claims in the realm

---

430,000 complete SARS-CoV-2 virus genomes have been submitted to the PubMed central database.

[18]   Countries affected by Covid-19: WHO Coronavirus (COVID-19) Dashboard. Accessed 30.12.2022.

[19]   Source map of countries with 5G networks: Statista, *Where 5G Technology Has Been Deployed*. Accessed 30.12.2022.

[20]   Work of Professor Andrew Wood in: Swinburne University of Technology, what 5G means for our health. Accessed 30.12.2022.

of conspiracy theories are sometimes supported by seemingly systematic approaches to uncover deceit regarding Covid-19 but unfortunately their way of tackling the information is completely misleading and full of mistakes[21]. Bearing in mind Popper's distinction between science and pseudoscience, one might question the label of theories on 5G networks causing Covid-19 as pseudoscientific since they seem to be easily verifiable and refutable as explained above. In fact, what is often the case with such popularised claims, which could be considered pseudoscientific, is that they are deliberately formulated in a way that makes them practically unfalsifiable, very often even by appealing to conspiracies or some allegedly scientific, yet unverifiable expertise.

Although one might think that the 5G theories of the origin of the disease do not equate to pseudoscience, particularly of the astrology type, but merely to faulty science, their claims bear striking similarities to those issued by the proponents of some of the pseudosciences. Namely, by citing conspiratorial elements behind its claims, the theory remains unverifiable and therefore, even more importantly, unfalsifiable. Hence, such conspiratorial claims have the same credo as pseudoscience: that they are not testable and demand belief. Along those conspiratorial lines, one of course might claim that the SARS-CoV-2 sequences entries are all faked which, bearing in mind their vast amount, involving hundreds of thousands of experts from many different countries, might

---

[21]   I hope that inquisitive readers will forgive me for not presenting more pseudo-theories, which are completely unfounded on facts, such as the conspiracy theory about vaccines carrying microchips.

seem a bit too paranoid, even for those who regard themselves as overly critical or sceptical. It is as if the claim science faces is that the real truth might be out there but is unreachable, whereby the only thing that remains is to devoutly believe in such claims.

The reason 5G network theory is such a clear example of a pseudo-theory is its deleterious effect on vaccination rates: if one believed there was no virus or that the immune system is simply weakened by 5G networks, one would think there would be no reason to get vaccinated. Other past examples of vaccine hesitancy include the infamous scare of the measles, mumps, and rubella (MMR) vaccine causing autism. Even though the claims from the original study were quickly rebutted and subsequently shown to be incorrect, leading to retraction of the manuscript[22], the scare still persisted. It would seem therefore appropriate that the public should be further educated in order to understand why the MMR study has been revoked, and not to hold that, if one were to continue along the conspiracy theories line, it is simply the vaccination lobby that managed to achieve its retraction as some of the opponents to vaccination might claim.

Such conflicting information could lead people to trust the simplest, more straightforward explanations, or evaluating the options of the SARS-CoV-2 virus or 5G network

---

[22] A very detailed review by DeStefano and Shimabukuro (2019) on the MMR vaccine controversy cites the initial study about the MMR vaccine causing autism by Wakefield et al. 1998, which was subsequently retracted. DeStefano and Shimabukuro provide details from a range of subsequent epidemiological studies, which have demonstrated that there is no correlation between the MMR vaccine and autism.

causing Covid-19 as having the same level of credibility, since they would not trust the verified authority on the matter. As a consequence, the public has less trust in scientists and medical doctors. The public might also have difficulties understanding that, while we are still learning about the virus and its new variants, the recommendations of the public health authorities are changing: a recommendation given at one point is revised a few months later. Therefore, those in doubt might simply conclude that since no one, including the medical experts, knows anything conclusive on the matter and they would not think they have any reason to trust anyone. Most worryingly of all, deliberate spreading of misinformation regarding vaccine safety further complicates the issue of trust in them[23].

From idleness to nihilism

The problem with vaccine hesitancy is not solely in the moral dimension—the responsibility we have for each other and the community as a whole—but also lies in the phenomenon of inertness, lack of action, and being uninterested in our broader social context. The phenomenon of the *sloth* in this case is reflected in unwillingness to get involved, not to think the conflicting issues through or to take the simpler

---

[23] One attempt at spreading misinformation was reported by two YouTubers who had been asked to spread unverifiable information about dangerous side effects of one of the vaccines; reported by Haynes and Carmichael, BBC, accessed 30.12.2022. Instead of agreeing to spread misinformation, the two YouTubers acted responsibly by warning the public about those who had approached them, revealing that such practices might happen on a much larger scale.

explanations for granted. A similar line of reasoning for the behaviour of many could be applicable elsewhere, whereby idleness would be seen as a strategy for indecisiveness and indifference on many other matters. One might find these comments too harsh since, after all, many of us are probably doing our best to navigate through the labyrinth of misinformation we face in our daily lives, let alone in a situation as serious as a pandemic. Yet, one might further note that the points above were not directed at anyone in particular, including those who vehemently opposed the vaccination, but rather simply tried to describe the inconsistencies and irrationalities which drive this and similar phenomena. After all, it might be that some particular situations, such as the stressful one of the Covid-19 pandemic, make most of us less cognitively apt by lulling us in our own echo chambers, where we might find more security and comfort. Personal choices are praised as the ultimate democratic goal and aspiration, making it seem as if even choices based on misinformation or refusal to contemplate some issues in depth have the same weight as those made in a more studious manner. To put the problem in a broader perspective one could say that, from a liberal perspective, one might be quite content with people having the opportunity to simply act, or not to act, as they choose to. However, the central question is if their decisions reflect their own informed choices or the situation is such that many people are rendered indifferent by the circumstances which would have led to their apathy, and hence could not have, or would unlikely have, chosen otherwise. Thus, it might appear that the prevailing liberal social context could have allowed the indifference in question to flourish.

The indifference and apathy described as being the by-product of the social context in modern times might seem an overly critical, perhaps slightly old-fashioned, standpoint to have, as if it were coming from one who would be critical of modern trends in general. Yet, these characteristics are closely associated with the phenomenon of nihilism, which was thoroughly described in the context of the developing modern age over a century ago. In particular, Friedrich Nietzsche described nihilism as rejection of everything worthwhile, meaningful or desirable, which arose from the constant swinging between the belief in the ultimate being, God, and rejection of everything[24]. Due to the rise of materialism, and with scientific explanations gaining more and more prominence in Western societies, Nietzsche considered Christian morality to have been the antidote for both practical and theoretical nihilism[25]. Namely, Christian churches propagated the idea that moral values have some supreme origin and were meaningful by having been derived from God. Yet, with the prominence of scientific and naturalistic explanations of the world around us, the religious

---

[24]   Nietzsche, *The Will to Power*, 11.

[25]   Nietzsche, *The Will to Power*, 16. Interestingly, Nietzsche talks about morality only in few instances, he refers explicitly to Christian teachings associated with it. Yet, in many other cases he does not explicitly mention any particular religion, although that is the impression one gets from his texts. He did not prepare his notes for publication; they were published after his death. Therefore, one cannot blame him for lack of specification and clarity. Nevertheless, bearing in mind these individual points in the context of the entire collection of notes and his other works, one can safely assume that Nietzsche did indeed think about the notion of morality in the sense it is used specifically in the Western Christian tradition.

explanations of meaning have lost their divinely superior character and value, and thereby become meaningless for a growing number of modern people.

What Nietzsche seems to have argued is that by providing more fine-grained, mechanistic, verifiable explanations of the natural phenomena, and the associated improvements in technologies which was a phenomenon people would have experienced and hence been aware of, the world would have somehow been seen as more banal and trivial and would have lost its divine, mystical character. He pointed out that *nihilism* arises when one seeks meaning but there is no meaning to be found. In other words, we delude ourselves that by providing causal, materialistic explanations we provide understanding of the world which, according to him, is clearly not the case[26]. Extending Nietzsche's ideas further one could say that with this constant search for meaning, after shunning away religious views and the alleged explanatory power of the transcendental, other positions such as mysticism and associated pseudoscience would have emerged as a means to compensate for the loss of meaning. Pseudoscience, similarly to religion, expects one to believe in what are supposedly inexplicable, unprovable and yet irrefutable matters, the ultimate meaning of which is beyond one's understanding but it is being revealed by some allegedly higher authority on the matter, it could be understood to provide certain comfort in knowing that we are all guided by some unknown forces of nature, not unlike the divine forces previously dispensed with, which are similarly not in our control.

---

[26]   Nietzsche, *The Will to Power*, 17-18, 357.

Thereby, pseudoscience could be said to be taking revenge on science, by attributing confused, supposedly scientific criteria to non-scientific concepts and beliefs. Since pseudoscientific claims are not appropriately testable nor verifiable, one can only believe in them: they are commonly told in the form of (mystical) stories and, as they cannot be falsified, they yearn to become dogmata.

With the rise of so many alternatives, faith in reliable, sound explanations is in decline. This would eventually lead the *sloth* to nihilism, as she or he would have less and less trust in science and reason. Yet, since we cannot dispense with science in the modern age, any faith-based position in the contemporary context compensates for it by being complemented with pseudoscience. Such a position seeks to utilise supposedly scientific terminology and concepts, thereby portraying itself as modern, although often still somewhat traditional, but nevertheless providing simplified and ultimately untrue explanations of the phenomena in question.

Engaging with the sloth

Whereas scientific positions have always relied on questioning and challenging with new ideas, those from pseudoscience or similar practices simply demand belief. Although the appeal of pseudoscientific claims might seem to be in democratising views and promoting plurality of opinions, by following the stance that every opinion is equally important they are over-trivialising the subject matter and leading to perpetuation of likely falsehoods. The poor sloth is faced with dogmatic beliefs perpetuated by pseudoscience; as these positions are often complemented by various ominous, sometimes threatening conspiracy theories regarding the official scientific findings, the sloth might also be sceptical about those as well and shun the sound, official explanations.

Finally, along the lines of the problem one commonly faces when deciding who or what explanations to trust, it might be beneficial to reflect on an interesting point Kant made regarding the contrast between dogma and scepticism. In particular, he praised the critical path of scientific method as one that represents the middle ground between dogmatism and scepticism[27]. It is perhaps not surprising that both dogmatism and scepticism are further emphasised and perverted by pseudoscience, since both require an equally firm position on belief and, in the case of pseudoscience, evade any significant critical reflection. Hence, the antidote would be the critical approach of scientific method which, even though it might not be available to all of us, provides us with the comfort of reliance on verifiable or, in Popper's terms, potentially falsifiable claims.

Thus, the middle ground for the sloth involves following the critical inquiry, the most demanding position of all, or relying on the sound explanations provided by those who would engage with the public in more informative and educational ways. The antidote to sloth is in questioning one's own beliefs, searching for possible justifications for them and trying to verify those one already holds in some meaningful way. Hence, this attempt at a critique is directed against sloth as a phenomenon, since the development of critical analytical skills is not something that is inborn but is developed by

---

[27] Kant, Critique of Pure Reason, 667.

educating people, preferably from the earliest age. One should be discouraged from making emotional instead of educated or rational choices on more serious matters: even though we are all entitled to either of those, one has to be aware that one also bears more responsibility in such social matters than solely for oneself and that a lot more thorough thinking is advisable in many cases.

Bibliography

Boylston, Arthur. (2012) The origins of inoculation. *J R Soc Med.* 105(7): 309–313.

Czajka, Hanna, Szymon Czajka, Paweł Biłas, Paulina Pałka, Szczepan Jędrusik and Anna Czapkiewicz. (2020) Who or What Influences the Individuals' Decision-Making Process Regarding Vaccinations? *Int J Environ Res Public Health*; 17(12): 4461.

Delany, J. (1912) Sloth. In *The Catholic Encyclopedia.* New York: Robert Appleton Company. Retrieved September 5, 2021 from New Advent: //www.newadvent.org/cathen/14057c.htm.

DeStefano, Frank and Tom T. Shimabukuro. (2019) The MMR Vaccine and Autism. *Annu Rev Virol*; 6(1): 585–600.

European Medicines Agency (EMA) press office. (07 April 2021) AstraZeneca's COVID-19 vaccine: EMA finds possible link to very rare cases of unusual blood clots with low blood platelets.   //www.ema.europa.eu/en/news/astrazenecas-cov id-19-vaccine-ema-finds-possible-link-very-rare-cases-unusu al-blood-clots-low-blood

Gardner, Alfred L. 2 March 2021. Sloth. *Encyclopaedia Britannica*, //www.britannica.com/animal/sloth. Accessed 13 September 2021.

Gettier, Edmund L. (1963) Is Justified True Belief Knowledge? *Analysis*. 23 (6): 121–123.

Haynes, Charlie and Flora Carmichael. (25 July 2021) The YouTubers who blew the whistle on an anti-vax plot. BBC. //www.bbc.com/news/blogs-trending-57928647

Hume, David. An Enquiry Concerning Human Understanding. From The Complete Works and Correspondence of David Hume. Electronic Edition. *InteLex Past Masters*. Accessed 28.09.2015.

Kant, Immanuel. (2007) *Critique of Pure Reason*. Penguin Classics. Translated and edited by Marcus Weigelt, original translation Max Müller.

Larson, Heidi J, Alexandre de Figueiredo, Zhao Xiahong, William S. Schulz, Pierre Verger, Iain G. Johnston, Alex R. Cook and Nick S. Jones. (2016) The State of Vaccine Confidence 2016: Global Insights Through a 67-Country Survey. *EBioMedicine*; 12: 295-301.

Nietzsche, Friedrich. (2017) *The Will to Power*. Penguin Classics. Translated by R. Kevin Hill and Michael A. Scarpitti, edited by R. Kevin Hill.

Plato, Meno. Translated by Benjamin Jowett. //classics.mit.edu/Plato/meno.html

Popper, Karl. (2005). The Logic of Scientific Discovery. Taylor & Francis e-Library. Author's translation with help from Dr. Julius Freed and Lan Freed.

Statista. 3.08.2021 Where 5G Technology Has Been Deployed. //www.statista.com/chart/23194/5g-networks-deployment-world-map/

Swinburne University of Technology. *What 5G means for our health*, Nature. //www.nature.com/articles/d42473-019-00009-7.

WHO Coronavirus (COVID-19) Dashboard. //covid19.who.int/table.

Yaqub, Ohid, Sophie Castle-Clarke, Nick Sevdalis and Joanna Chataway. (2014) Attitudes to vaccination: a critical review. *Review Soc Sci Med*; 112: 1-11.

SUPERBIA
The Manual of Virtue Signalling

Josette Baer

What is virtue signalling (VS)? According to The Cambridge Dictionary online, virtue signalling is "an attempt to show other people that you are a good person, for example by expressing opinions that will be acceptable to them, especially on social media: Virtue signalling is the popular modern habit of indicating that one has virtue merely by expressing disgust or favour for certain political ideas or cultural happenings".[1]

One could argue that VS is an older social, and historical phenomenon, originating in unfree regimes that forced the individual to declare consent with the ruler, monarch, or Party president in public, for all to witness, regardless of the individual's opinion. Thus, the public demonstration of consent that is required to survive in an oppressive regime. Yet, a closer look at historical regimes teaches us that VS is, indeed, a socio-political phenomenon of the digital age, our times. Why?

If I clap my hands at a meeting of the Soviet Communist Party in Moscow in the 1930s, demonstrating my agreement with whatever Stalin has just "suggested", I am not virtue signalling. I clap because everybody else does, and if I don't, the chances that I will end up in a labour camp are high. The

---

[1]   https://dictionary.cambridge.org/dictionary/english/virtue-signalli ng; accessed 5 May 2023.

116   Josette Baer

GULAG (*glavnoe upravlenie lagerei*) was the system of labour camps established by Stalin. My not clapping indicates to the totalitarian leader that I dissent—not a good idea if I want to stay alive and protect my family. The same applies to the people of North Korea: watching the funeral of the late Kim Yongil (1941–2011), I observed how the masses were crying, jumping up and down, waving their hands, wiping their tears away, while each person tried to top the others in his or her show of grief.[2]

Again, this is not VS; I think that this is not only obedient behaviour that complies with the social norms of the Chuch'e Sasang,[3] the religious personality cult of North Korea and its family-church leaders. To us, it is something much worse: the fear of a people of being accused by the totalitarian authorities of not showing enough grief, of not being in line. I think it is a blend of mass hysteria, fear, brainwashing, but also political conviction of citizens who have lived for generations in this political system.

What is VS today, to us? I think, it is a new psychological phenomenon of the 21st century, since it has developed on social media, which offer the following advantages: one can publish one's likes or dislikes in seconds on Twitter or Instagram and thus become or remain a member of a virtual group. The 21st century activist/virtue signaller does not have to argue, to reason; she does not have to prove that she has thought things through, nor does she need to prove that

---

[2]   https://www.youtube.com/watch?v=JSLnuos5pkw; accessed 8 September 2023.
[3]   https://www.jstor.org/stable/23622341; accessed 9 September 2023.

she is qualified to have an opinion. It suffices to join the 'moral' crowd and agree with the 'ethical' arguments of a group, on whatever topic. The theme or content of 'debates', which are no debates at all, but rather exclamative echo chambers, is not the point; what is important is my show of consent. Likes, not actions. Go with the group, do not think, do not be critical—that is why VS is fostering totalitarian thought, prompting uber obedient, intolerant and pluralism-resistant behaviour to an extent hitherto unknown in the Free West.

Also, the political activist thinks that he or she is acting out of free will; in fact, one is caving into peer pressure. This raises the perennial question where one's freedom begins and ends. To what extent am I psychologically manipulated when I engage in liking or disliking? Blessed is he and she, who is aware of those dangers and stays away from social media.

As a virtue-signaller, I can jump on any cultural or political bandwagon; it doesn't matter if I believe in the credo, catechisms or arguments. The main motivation is to join a group. I do not even have to understand the theme or issue at stake. The key principle of VS is that I engage in an exclamative fashion: I clap online, demonstrating my consent. On social media, I can be perfectly ignorant and have a voice at the same time. In this regard, the web is very democratic: every Tom, Dick and Harry, or Barbie, Jane, and Marjorie—a nod towards the equality of the sexes here—can demonstrate how kind and moral they are while doing nothing at all. A like—and you are fine.

I think that the principal motive of VS is the deep-seated wish to be a member of something, a group, a movement, a conviction to make the world a better place. It is the wish to be acknowledged, to have family, to join others. If I am right, then the origins of VS are an individual's loneliness. Individuals enjoying and embracing solitude have no need to demonstrate their views in the virtual world. They are happy on their own, without constantly demonstrating their morality on social media.

Hermann Lübbe (*1926), professor of political philosophy, a neo-Kantian and my teacher back in the 1990s at Zurich University, summarized and defined the origins of political correctness. What we today refer to as VS is an aspect of political correctness, a fascinating mode of behaviour, "the triumph of attitude versus reason".[4] Attitude does not require research, nor reason; one can always be on the 'correct' side in any discussion by performing the attitude one believes the group shall approve of. The application of Reason, in Kant's terms, however, means thinking things through; it requires effort, reflection, research. Words come cheap, thinking things through, not so. Today, to speak up, to voice one's critical opinion, is to be punished with social cancelling.

Grandma Betty is calling granddaughter Izzy who lives in affluent Palo Alto, California. Izzy's dad Joke, Betty's son, has made his wealth in the IT industry in Silicon Valley. Betty is calling Izzy from her top-level apartment in San Francisco:

---

4   Hermann Lübbe, *Politischer Moralismus. Der Triumph der Gesinnung über die Urteilskraft* (Berlin: Siedler, 1989 (6)).

Betty: "Izzy, it's grandma. I saw you on TV, on our local channel VRTSIG this morning—the demonstration and the window-smashing at our best department stores downtown. What were you thinking? And why were you wearing that rainbow T-shirt, looking like a Cali surfer girl in the 1970s? Last time I checked we are in 2023."

Izzy: "Hi Granny. It was a demonstration in support of trans people."

Betty: "Who are these trash people? Never heard of them."

Izzy: "No, Granny, it's TRANS, T-R-A-N-S, human beings who want to change their gender—I can't believe you've never heard of them! We have to protect their rights as a sexual minority, make sure that their rights are protected by the law as human rights."

Betty: "What minority rights? And why is this about sex? I thought that the black people got their civil rights back in 1968. I was in Wash to support Dr. Martin Luther King. A fine walk that was, indeed. I also paid to support the Stonewall movement. Gay people are US citizens like everybody else."

Izzy: "Granny, that was ages ago. The gay people are recognized today, yes, but mankind must make more progress. We are concerned today with TRANS people: they need our support, and you, with your wealth, could help us: please pay 1 million dollars into our account, so we can make sure everybody wanting to trans can do so."

Betty: "What? 1 million? That's a lot of money. Why do these trash people need so much money?"

Izzy: "Ok granny, I am being very patient now, let me explain this to you a second time: they need the money to change their gender, to find their true identity. You can help to make the world a better place, to make a difference. Paypal is the safest way, please transfer the money today."

Betty: "Making the world a better place? I thought that was seeking peace, to come to an understanding with the Soviets, to deter nuclear war. And what does gender mean? In my times, we just called it sex. And we enjoyed it, especially in the war, when you didn't know if you'd live another day."

Izzy: "Wow. Yeah, as I have said: ages ago. But still, could you post on Twitter that you are supporting our cause?"

Betty: "Twitter? Why are you talking about birds now? I can't even remember my own telephone number, so why should I go on that Twitter thing to send you money, to support a cause I still don't understand?"

Izzy: "To be authentic, Granny, to be on the ethically right side. Otherwise, people might think you are discriminating against trans people."

Betty: "Being authentic? How much more authentic can you be than fighting the Nazis and the Japanese? In WWII, your granddad was in the Pacific, and I was in Hong Kong as a secret liaison officer with the British and the Soviets. And how could I possibly discriminate against people I've never met? Don't lecture me on morals, my dear."

Izzy: "Gran, I have to dash soon to a meeting of our TRANS support group. Please arrange for the transfer to be done today. We really need the money."

Betty: "Ok, so you want me to pay USD 1 million into the Paypal account of your associates who then forward it to the trash people to have their biological sex changed. And my money will make a difference. I also should post this donation on Twitter so that everybody knows about my generous gift? Is that right?"

Izzy: "Yes, granny, you are spot on. Now, can we count on your donation?"

Betty: "Frankly, my dear, no. Get yourself a job and then you can support any group to your liking, with your own money."

Izzy: "But Granny, that is so unfair of you. These people really need any support they can get. I am taking gender studies at UCLA; I don't have the time to work a job."

Izzy: "Granny, can we count on your donation?"

Izzy: "Granny, are you still there?"

EPILOGUE
The Seven Slovak Sorrows

Jozef Banáš

I was delighted and honoured when Josette Baer approached me to write a reflection on the subject of the seven deadly sins. At first, I wondered if I had the right to ponder this metaphysical topic, but finally I thought who else from Slovakia could do it? I calculated how many of us Slovaks are able to work, and it turned out that I am the only one who can do it. The following calculation proves my point; you, dear reader, will not only get an idea of how many people live here, but also an answer to the question why Slovakia is where she is. Look at the following figures:

Population of Slovakia (2011 census): **5,538,036**
Of which, juveniles under the age of 15: -830,439
working remainder: **4,707,597**
Of these, pensioners over 65: -672,724
working remainder: **4,034,873**
Of this, the unemployed: -376,270
working remainder: **3,658,603**
Of these, ethnic minorities: -506,738
working remainder: **3,152,265**
Of these, secondary school students: -221,374
working remainder: **2,930,891**
Of these, university students: -188,885
working remainder: **2,742,006**

Of this, civil servants (officials): -343,560

working remainder: **2,398,446**

Of these, alcoholics: -312,854

working remainder: **2,085,592**

Of these, Slovaks working abroad: -155,800

working remainder: **1,929,792**

Of these, idlers: -1,723,456

working remainder: **206,336**

Of these, those unfit for work: -74,375

working remainder: **131,961**

Of these, service personnel, including civilian employees of armed forces: -21,500

working remainder: **110,461**

Of these, convicted and imprisoned criminals: -10,204

working remainder: **100,257**

Of these, deputies (municipal, district, regional, NR SR, EP): -24,897

working remainder: **75,360**

Of these, schizophrenics: (24,176.5 x 2) 48,353

working remainder: **27,007**

Of these, psychopaths: 19,657

working remainder: **7,350**

Of these, parish priests of both confessions: -5,199

working remainder: **2,151**

Of which philatelists: -2,076

working remainder: **75**

Of which ministers and state secretaries: -39

working remainder: **36**

Of these, the Slovak national ice hockey squad: -35

The final working remainder is **1—and that would be me.**

So, my friends, you will surely acknowledge that even if I didn't want to, there is no one else in Slovakia who could write a reflection on our seven Slovak sins, and not only our mortal sins. However, I have altered the assignment a bit. The patron saint of Slovakia is the Virgin Mary of the Seven Sorrows—I will return to her later—and I have taken the liberty of calling my work *The Seven Slovak Sorrows*. In Catholic Slovakia, it is unimaginable that our patron saint could be the Virgin Mary of the Seven Sins.

I have travelled the world, and it truly upsets me that people confuse us with Slovenia, the Czech Republic and even with the Hungarians, although it is true that we lived with these nations for many centuries in one common constitutional monarchy.

For a better understanding of our destiny, I shall give you the example of my mother. She was born in Austria-Hungary, then lived in the first Czechoslovak Republic, then in the autonomous Slovak state under the Tiso regime, at Hitler's beck and call, then in Hungary, then for a while again in democratic Czechoslovakia. After savouring the following forty years in communist Czechoslovakia, she lived briefly again in democratic Czechoslovakia, then found herself once more in an independent Slovak state. She survived eight state regional divisions and regimes. What is remarkable about her seemingly nomadic life is that she never left her native village near Bratislava. This is the name of the capital of our country today. At the time of her birth, it was called Pozsonyi, or Pressburg. So, you certainly understand why we Slovaks live huddled in our vales and dales, waiting every moment for someone to invade our territory again from the north, southeast or west. Despite everything, we have survived and are managing quite well, mainly thanks to our mountains and forests, in which we have always successfully hidden away. However, the situation is getting worse, the forests are shrinking, and I fear that we'll end up like the Sahara. The world will never know that this desert was once a training ground for Slovak lumberjacks.

If you want to understand any state, you have to start with its history, even if it isn't certain which history is the right one, since every winner of a war or revolution dictates what is going to be written in school history books. Slovakia is no exception, although it is surprising that we have a history of our own at all. It is brief, but all the more intense. After all, a state positioned at one of the main crossroads of world events cannot have a dull history.

We are one of the youngest countries in the world. The making of our state succeeded at the third attempt. We tried the first time on March 14, 1939, and that ended on May 8, 1945. We made the second attempt on January 1, 1969, when we declared the autonomy of the Slovak Socialist Republic within the political framework of the Czechoslovak Socialist Republic. This ended on March 1, 1990. Our third attempt was on January 1, 1993. Before that third, last and successful attempt, we carefully—after thorough scrutiny of the political developments around us—went out into the streets, rattling our keys to demand freedom. That was the famous Velvet Revolution of November 1989. We had yet to learn that the fundamental fallacy of history attributes revolutions to those who started them. It is increasingly clear to us now that those who end revolutions are the ones who matter in the long run. Like the Parisians in July 1789, we succumbed to a feeling of victory in November 1989, forgetting that both the fall of the Bastille and the Central Committee of the Communist Party were only opening shots.

We expected many things from the coup, another name for the Velvet Revolution; unfortunately, as is our tradition, we kept our heads down, and only the bravest were willing to do something for the motherland, the nation. From that November on, it has become a tradition that people who haven't really achieved anything else go into politics. Those who don't even dare to do that are afraid that we could go back to where we were before the revolution. Ranting and railing, the feeling of powerlessness. We don't want to admit that we condemn the powerful because we don't have the opportunity to gain power ourselves. And we don't admit at all— fortunately, not only us Slovaks, but also other post-communist states in Central Europe—that most of the dirty things in history have happened not because of the boldness of the power-hungry, but because of the cowardice of those whose duty it would have been to resist them.

No, we don't have to be heroes or martyrs or dissidents. It is enough to be decent. Nobody has the right to judge his neighbour until he has walked in his shoes.

I belong to the generation of those Slovak citizens, who entered the workforce in the 1970s and 1980s; that means that we were used to meandering and zig-zagging to survive in the regime referred to as "real Socialism" or "actually existing Socialism". We just wanted to look at ourselves in the mirror, without feelings of guilt and shame, and look our children in the eye, not forsaking human decency in difficult circumstances and a difficult political environment. We were no heroes, but we tried to be decent people, do our daily work and fulfil our parental duties and, if possible, not stand out from the crowd. Invisibility and obedience saved professional futures.

Who was a hero? One well-known priest who served nine years in the communist prison in Jáchymov told me that he was no hero, because he did not go to prison out of free will. Before his arrest, Jesus too, in fear, begged God to "let this cup pass". We examine the past of our nation even in the institutions intended for it. When I once talked to the German chancellor Willy Brandt (1913–1992) about how the Germans coped with their past, he told me, "We've had experts and institutes for researching the past, but you can't learn the circumstances, reasons and motives of a person's actions from papers. The surest way to find out how someone behaved in the past is to watch how they behave today." I agree with Brandt. He who was decent and honest during totalitarianism is decent and honest in a democracy too, and he who was a fraud, thief and liar during totalitarianism is one today. All the more so, because today the government does not force anybody into wrongdoing. This applies especially to young journalist-blowhards who like to lecture us on how they would have behaved heroically under socialism, if, of course, they had lived under socialism...

We don't have to participate in the process of political progress unconditionally, it suffices not to hinder it. There is no obligation to be at the forefront of efforts to bring about tolerance, but it is embarrassing to blunder in right at the end. A dictatorship with the old dogmas is already in the making. Such a situation is all the more dangerous because it disguises the old dogmas under the masks of respectability and credibility. And the new packaging can easily tempt those who fiercely hold a tiny certainty in their hands. They know that a pigeon is better, but to catch it we must first release the sparrow from the palms of our hands. This "first" is the hardest step. Fear of this first step equals revolutions that failed.

To me, the existence of various political parties and movements is not a proof of the search for truth, but an effort to convince others of my convictions and opinions. Therefore, the decisive factor for liberty, i.e. political freedom, is not democracy as a system and constitution, but human tolerance. For the fisherman, the fishing rod is an absolute truth; for the fish, the open water. When I think that even the Enlightenment philosopher Voltaire (François-Marie Arouet, 1694–1778) fought against the Catholic Church under the slogan "Stifle the beast", I am not a great optimist. The vast majority of "successful" politicians entered the scene at a stage when the enthusiasm of the first revolutionaries was already vanishing. However, they do not realize that their rise to power is also the beginning of their fall. A permanent, internal law of power is that whoever achieves it, feels that he has achieved his goal. He switches off his efforts, telling himself that the triumph is already his. He doesn't notice that new fighters are already diligently training. Therefore, it is the weak who struggle for power because they don't have the strength for a lifelong struggle with themselves. They can muster strength only to fight the enemy.

So, here we have the **first Slovak sorrow**: we have come to believe that the most important people in a revolution are those who start it and not those who end it.

At the time of completing this essay, in the summer of 2022, the sovereign Slovak Republic still exists, which is already a record. We are fulfilling the prophetic words of one of our more significant writers, Pavel Vilikovský, who wrote:

> "All nations want to plough a deep furrow into the history of mankind, they want to surpass themselves. Although they have yet to tread on one another's heels, only the Slovaks, God's children, see the meaning and fulfilment of their existence in that they exist. Who else can be so innocently happy as a child: a hundred years have passed and we're still here! So we haven't lived in vain! We are, surely it can't be just this! And immediately filled with enthusiasm, we set a clear goal: Let's be more!"

It is said that the father of the first Slovakia was Andrej Hlinka, the father of the second Gustáv Husák and the third Vladimír Mečiar. Aware of the complex mental situation of this country, I am more and more convinced that none of these gentlemen could have been fathers of Slovakia. It had to be someone fallible and relatively incompetent. Or he had too much work and slacked off a bit. It seems to me this could be God or someone acting on his behalf. I have a bad feeling that during the creation of Slovakia, God was somewhat tired, so he gave instructions to a deputy. He assigned this task to a research institute, which apparently entrusted one of its numerous branches with the creation of Slovakia. In the end, the creation of our country was left to some subordinate heavenly angel, who, like France and Great Britain in Munich in 1938, characteristically ignored us. That a heavenly commission took over Slovakia, with all its additional shortcomings, is proof to me that God really does look a lot like mankind. We did not, as is the norm in the history of international relations, set our borders ourselves; other states determined them for us. We were placed in a free space between Poland, Ukraine, Hungary, Austria and the Czech Republic, although it is believed that there were a few madcaps who objected: it would be better if we Slovaks were in New Zealand, fulfilling the most typical desire of our nation—to hole up and enjoy a blessed peace as far away as possible from everything.

We probably had a weak influence on the powerful in the world at the time, that is why today we have to fight not only our neighbours—this is so unfair! New Zealand doesn't have any!—but also deal with Hungarians, Czechs, Poles, Roma, Ruthenians, Germans, Záhoraks, Koňars, Vraňars, Prešpuráks and a few Jews (although there aren't many of them, they're everywhere) and many others. However, the fact that you have many neighbours does not have to be a burden. You can choose one to join. Or vice versa, a neighbour can choose you. If it turns out that the neighbour you've chosen or who's chosen you wasn't the best choice, you can turn away from them. Fortunately, in history, we have always managed to join the winners in due time. Then, we have always showed our gratitude to the winners, that we were able to win with them and conveniently forget which side we were on before. For a small state, being at the side of a big one has an indisputable advantage. You can turn away at the right moment and pretend that you just happened to be in their vicinity.

Fighting at the side of a big and influential state was and still is a key strategy of the Slovak and former Czechoslovak army. We have become so used to acting as a flank in our history that we can hardly imagine the defensive capability of our army if fighting on our own. Being at someone's side has a huge advantage. If the person you have joined is the winner, you will at least get to lick some of the cream. However, if that person loses, you can just turn away at the right moment and the loser will have to swallow what is coming to him on his own. Twice in history, we have turned away in time: in 1918 and 1945. Consequently, we Slovaks ended up on the side of the winners, despite having our ears cut off. As can be seen from these newspaper comments we have always felt good on the flank. The first comment describes the exercise of the armies of the Warsaw Pact, known as "Shield", *Ščit* in Russian, in 1982:

"Soldiers of the Czechoslovak People's Army, side by side with the armies of the Soviet Union and our allies, demonstrate their readiness to defend peace on the battlefield. The task of the exercise is to harmonize the combat activity of individual armies and types of troops, to check the level of operational-tactical training of the staffs, the level of training of soldiers and commanders to strengthen the close international cooperation of fraternal armies."

The second comment is also about the Shield exercise, but this time under the English name Shield 2015 and, for a change, it is an exercise of the NATO armies in Slovakia:

> "It is a series of training activities aimed at testing all levels of command of the armed forces. The exercise simulates possible threats that our armed forces must be prepared for in the short and medium term. The armed forces at all levels will have the opportunity to practice their skills in non-military operations, as well as combat situations in the defence of Slovakia with the support of NATO member countries."

The advantage of staying on the flank is that you cannot lose. Thanks to this attitude, the Slovak army distinguishes itself by the fact that it is the only army in the world that, throughout its history, has not lost a single war, not a single battle, not even a single skirmish. It has achieved this unique feat by never fighting alone. We believe that our boys and girls in green will succeed in maintaining this tradition for as long as possible. However, in the history of our army, there were also moments when our soldiers were faced with significant losses, but in the end, it did not happen. The soldiers left before the battle started. They fled on horses, wagons, carriages, cars and most often in the traditional Slovak way, i.e. on foot. Naturally, they fled only in situations where Slovak politicians had not signed a capitulation, that is, when reasons for fleeing were obvious. In the event that capitulation was not signed, Slovak groups deserted or went over to the enemy.

However, to be fair, we did have some significant losses. In 1918, we capitulated to the Russians, French, and British; the joy of this capitulation was somewhat spoiled by the Hungarians and Austrians, who capitulated with us; because of Milan R. Štefánik's (1880–1919) *legia* that fought in Russia and Siberia, the victors forgave us our defeat. Twenty years later, we capitulated to the Germans, but again, unfortunately, we were not allowed fully fledged joy, because the Czechs and, indirectly, the French and British also capitulated with us. However, we made up for it in 1944, when we fought the Germans in the Slovak National Uprising. In 1968, we could not enjoy the independence of our capitulation to the Soviets either, because, unfortunately, the Czechs also capitulated with us.

So, **the second Slovak sorrow:** in history and with hindsight, it has turned out that we have almost always been on the wrong side.

It is obvious that if you want to get to know not only our country better, but any country, you must visit. If you want to come to Slovakia, you have to find it, and that is not always easy. Sometimes, people confuse us with Slovenia, sometimes with the Czech Republic, or we simply cannot be found just because nobody confuses us with somebody else. That is why our representatives should carry maps and show where we are, at every appropriate and inappropriate opportunity abroad. There is nothing to be done—foreign countries just have to get used to us. This is easy because like most countries we also have four cardinal directions.

Slovakia's geographical location is at the crossroads of the Western and Eastern European cultures; this position has also dramatically influenced the differences between the western and eastern parts of our country. The basic difference between the two parts is that the sun rises earlier in the east than in the west. The west of the east of Slovakia logically starts at the eastern end of the village of Východná (Slovak for "east") and continues to the Ukrainian border. Conversely, the east of the west begins at the western end of the village of Východná and ends at the Moravian border. Due to the fact that the sun is highest at noon, of which they have the most in central Slovakia, the most sunburnt Slovaks are the Central Slovaks.

In ancient times, people came to Slovakia on wagons, horses, carriages, rafts, ponies, but in the times of the Inquisition also on witches' brooms, which sometimes outnumbered the inquisitors. In less ancient times, some came to Slovakia in armoured personnel carriers or tanks. As for Slovaks, in most cases they came to Slovakia to be born here. They are born in maternity hospitals, but sometimes also in other places, for example, at home, in a car, in a field, or even in a foundling's rescue point. There are areas in Slovakia where babies are still born in storks' nests. If you want to get out of Slovakia, it is the same procedure: you just go in the other direction.

Every nation has not only a nationality, but also a mission. The primary mission of the Slovaks is to suffer and in the breaks between suffering to suffer anew. The Slovak natural tendency to suffer is also reflected in its poetry: "Only have three words in your heart—love, suffer and forgive." In our country, suffering has always been considered a virtue. More precisely, the suffering of other people. Suffering oneself is not that popular. Suffering is a fundamental activity that has been required of Slovaks in history in every era and under every regime. Priests even built their existence on it. When it seemed to the Kaloč archbishop Patačič during the Austria-Hungary period that the Slovaks had not suffered enough, he had twelve canes cut for everyone just for being Slovak. For sure. When Ľudovít Štúr (1815–1856) proposed "eternal redemption" and the abolition of serfdom at the Hungarian Diet in 1847 on behalf of the Slovaks, another Slovak, Ľudovít Košút, later known as Kossuth Lajos (1802–1894), rebuked him with the words: "The deputy of the royal city of Zvolen is a fantasist. Suffering is the doom and destiny of the people."

If suffering is the mission of the Slovak man, it is also the mission of the Slovak woman. Even more so, because she does not suffer and did not just suffer under the yoke of the Hungarians, Czechs, Jews, Tatars, Turks—from contemporary sources it appears that some Slovak women suffered quite pleasantly under the Turks—and, of course, also under the Slovak yoke. The average Slovak is convinced that he is a member of the only nation in the world that suffers. That is also why the patron saint of predominantly Catholic Slovakia is the Seven-Sorrowed Virgin Mary. Even the day, 15 September, when we remember the seven sorrows of the Virgin Mary, is a national holiday. We look forward to it because we do not have to go to work, and we do not mind at all that the vast majority of Slovak Catholics have no idea what Mary's seven sorrows are and why we remember them on 15 September.

The third Slovak sorrow is the feeling that we are the only nation in the world that suffers.

In 1989, I was one of those who, on the revolutionary platforms of the November squares, promised people a beautiful tomorrow when we would get rid of the totalitarian communist regime. Today, it is thirty-three years since the revolution, and I am glad that people no longer remember my appearances back then. I would have never thought that thirty-three years after the fall of communism, we would be dealing with the problems of rising prices, inflation, lack of heat and energy, hopelessness, hypocrisy, hatred, poverty, insecurity, cultural and educational decline. After the fall of communism, access to the treasures of world culture, which had been supposedly concealed from us, seemed to be within reach. I have randomly selected the most watched programmes of Slovak television and the cinema programmes in Bratislava's Au Park. They eloquently illustrate the fruitful presence, diversity, and richness of the treasures of world cinema on today's screens:

Television Markíza, programme of 24 August (or any other day):
6.00 Dr. House, US series
7.55 Alf, US comedy series
8.30 Step by Step, US comedy series
12.40 She's the Man, US romantic comedy
14.35 Surf's Up, US animated film
16.15 Love, Weddings and Other Disasters, US romantic comedy
20.30 The Bounty Hunter, comedy USA
23.00 Hunt to Kill, action film USA
01.00 The Bounty Hunter, comedy USA

02.40 Smallville, US action series

Television also includes Slovak advertising in its artistic programmes, so domestic creative production does not lose out.
I could present television programmes day after day. Try to
guess from which country they originate.

**Films screened in Bratislava's Au Park on July 6 (or any other
day):**
Terminator Genesis, action film, USA
Ted 2, comedy, USA
Forever Young, romantic film, USA
Localfilmis Slovakia; Woman in Gold, drama, USA
Danny Collins, comedy, USA
Wow, comedy, USA
Unfriended, horror, USA
Dark Places, thriller, USA
Jurassic World, adventure film, USA

Where has my youth under totalitarianism gone, when it was
obvious to us that, in addition to American, there were also
German, Polish, French, Czech, Slovak, Russian, Hungarian,
Spanish, Swedish, Austrian, Yugoslav films and cinema productions from other countries?

The destruction of national roots continues at an unprecedented pace. Since the Gentle Revolution, we have ceased
to be peasants and housewives and become farmers, we no
longer have news but headlines, laws in the National (!)
Council are not made, but "created;" we don't say any longer
"prepáč", but "sorry;" instead of "dobre", we say OK and we

no longer show surprise as did our famous actors, Satinský and Lasica, when they used to exclaim "fíha!", but we show a dumbfounded stare and rolling eyeballs exclaiming "Wow"! In the Avion shopping centre, they did not open a "Dom detí", but a "Kid's House"; we no longer have Cinderella, Valibuks, Janko Hraško, Little Red Riding Hood, Sleeping Beauty, but MacQueens, Macgyver, Barbies, Shreks and Alfs. Slavic holidays have been replaced by more modern ones, such as St. Valentine's and other American holidays that have become extremely hollow BS, sorry, Halloween. Even the "Prvá slovenská krčma" in Bratislava is called "The First Slovak Pub."

I wrote a novel, Velestúr, based on a mythical hill in the Kremnické region; the name is a combination of the names of the Slavic goddess Veles and the god Tur. For now, that hill is still called Velestúr. If you want to enjoy it, you had better visit there now, because it may soon be called Wheeliestour. And instead of the "Vysoké Tatry", we will inevitably have the High Tatras. Equally, the greeting "spánombohom" has been replaced with the trendy "Good luck." The limitless Americanization of our life is increasingly affecting the younger generation, which is already almost convinced that the only culture in the world is American and is impatiently waiting for the moment when the famous robber Juraj Jánošík will become Georgie Johnny Chic.

According to Wikipedia, patriotism is love and devotion to the homeland, pride in its past and present and efforts to protect the interests of the homeland. A patriot is a person who feels national pride. An expression of patriotism is, for example, singing the national anthem. I know many people who are bad singers but good patriots. Our patriotism flares up most prominently at football and ice hockey matches. Especially if we have won and carry on winning. If we beat the opposition, we happily evaluate the match in the first-person plural: "But we gave it to them", "We were better", "They had nothing on us" and the like. If we lose the match, we distance ourselves from our athletes and transfer the evaluation of the lost match to the third person plural: they are no longer ours, they are no longer us, but them: "But they gave it to them", "They didn't have anything on them", "They went to sleep on the pitch". During the matches of our football teams with foreign countries, the sequence of the weakening of patriotism takes place in this algorithm:

0 : 0—we are encouraged, and a cautious patriotism prevails

1 : 0—we are even more encouraged; patriotism is increasing although we are still sitting down

2 : 0—we cheer enthusiastically, patriotism lifts us from our seats

2 : 1—we are encouraged 30 percent less, the greater patriots are standing, the lesser have sat down

2 : 2—we are encouraged 60 percent less, everyone has sat down

2 : 3—we are silent, we are starting to prepare for the defeat that we secretly expected all along

2 : 4—we encourage the opponent, we whistle at our own team, making it demonstratively clear that we have nothing in common with those useless bums in white and blue jerseys.

The most amazing thing about our patriotism is that even if we wanted to be patriots, we have nobody to express patriotism towards, since nothing in Slovakia belongs to Slovaks anymore. Even our most famous football club Slovan Bratislava no longer belongs to Slovaks. The owner may be Slovak, but several players have no clue in which country they are actually playing. It was touching to watch the Hungarian and Slovak fans during a match between Slovan and the most famous Hungarian club, Ferencváros Budapest. Both fan camps proudly waved the Slovak and Hungarian flags, as they should, they threw firecrackers at each other, swore at each other and after the match bravely fought with each other, in the English manner. It was remarkable that two Hungarians started the fight for Ferencváros and two Slovaks for Slovan. The others were from Mali, Morocco, Bosnia, Norway, Nigeria, Georgia, Ivory Coast, Suriname, Brazil, England and other countries.

So, I would call **the fourth Slovak sorrow** the gradual loss of national roots.

I do not come from a family that enjoyed material well-being under the old regime. In our house, we were among the last to own a television set. At first, I was excited that I did not have to go around begging the neighbours to let me watch TV, but after a while I started to feel lonely. The other boys with whom I used to watch football matches together at the Dorotkos, Pobežals or Dutkos were in a similar situation. When there were broadcasts of more important sports events, such as the World Cup in Chile in 1962, even the grown-ups came to the lucky owner of a TV, and in one living room twenty neighbours would cheer for our team. We also spent time watching hockey matches together or watched the figure skating competitions of the Romanov siblings and Karol Divín with excitement. We rejoiced and grieved together, our fathers drank wine from sadness or joy, which was always brought by one of the neighbours. Usually, several people brought wine. It happened that the celebration of some victories or drowning the sorrow of defeats lasted until the late hours of the evening. Sometimes our mothers also joined, an initially innocent-looking transmission, perhaps from a Spartakiad, turned into the strengthening of neighbourly relations.

In the winter, fathers watered the yards together and created ice rinks for their children, and in the summer, they even played volleyball tournaments with their children. Parents knew about each other's problems; they borrowed eggs, coffee, cigarettes, or money from each other a few days before payday. Today, we no longer borrow eggs. The shelves of the stores are stacked with loads of goods, but we have stopped greeting each other. Actually, there's no one to greet, because we have no idea who in the block of flats is our neighbour. We take the elevator to the garage, get into the car and go to work. Sometimes we treat ourselves to a meeting with friends in a café, where we put on our headphones, pull out our laptop or handle urgent phone calls and text messages. We sit with a girlfriend or boyfriend, who during the meeting also takes care of text messages or just browses the web. We return to the garage, get into the elevator and anonymously enter our apartment, where our children are waiting for us, surfing on the computer or watching an action thriller on the most modern 3D TV receiver -- or worse, silly videos of their peers on YouTube. They do not notice your arrival and so as not to disturb them, you carefully disappear to a nearby inn, where you and your equally neglected neighbours reminisce about the golden days when you didn't have a TV at home. We've turned into consumers who organize their daily habits in accordance with advertising. I refuse to be a consumerist idiot, I got tired of all the praise of washing powders, medicines, serums, cars, booze, chocolate, toothpaste, and soft-hearted banks. I pulled myself together, put on my headphones, found some great relaxing music on the internet that brought me to the alpha level. I was feeling good, my soul flying like a feather through the heavenly gardens of space, when the angelic music of the harp was drowned out by a strong male voice informing me that this winter would be really special, full of dangers, but I could negotiate it safely with tyres with maximum braking power. I flinched, my heart pounding, but I managed to return to the alpha level.

As soon as I started to breathe calmly, I was jolted again, almost convulsed by the sound of the engine of a van from the new generation of vehicles most suitable for my business. Then some idiot tried to persuade me to show up on the ski slopes in the most fashionable style and feel as comfortable as possible. My heart rate rose to one hundred and twenty, I started to panic, I felt deep down that I was starting to hate advertising, its producers, clients and broadcasters. Since I have started relaxing, I have been mean, I refuse to talk to people, it makes me want to murder. My psychiatrist advised me to stop watching commercials and relax. Where? I asked. Put on some good relaxing music, there's plenty of it on the internet: it has made me happy. At that moment, I lost control and hit the psychiatrist with a heavy object. I don't know if he survived, but I was greatly relieved.

I recognized **the fifth Slovak sorrow**: we have stopped being people and turned into consumers and breeders of new consumers.

The big ailment of our country is bureaucracy. Its traditions go back to the times of the Austro-Hungarian empire. It developed significantly during communist times and has reached gigantic proportions since our entry into the European Union. Fifty years ago, when a construction worker needed to attach a number plate to a new building, he took two nails and banged them in. It took him a minute. Ten years later, in a similar situation, he had to go to the construction foreman, who, for a bribe in the form of a bottle of beer and a bread roll with garlic sausage, agreed to the nailing of the number plate. In 1980, the worker then had to go to the foreman and the foreman to the construction manager, who discussed the problem of the board with the director and finally, after some two hours, he received the approval to nail on the plate. In 1990, the investor would have to bid for the nailing of the board and, after a week's evaluation, he chose the cheapest of the three offers so that the worker would nail on the plate after payment of the invoice. In 2000, the construction manager would have to ask for approval from the director of the construction company, who would choose the cheapest out of the five offers prescribed by law. However, he would invoice the work at the price of the most expensive, as he would include a thirty percent commission. After payment of the invoice, the worker could nail on the plate—after two months. In 2010, six years after our entry into the European Union, the construction worker would choose a foreman, the construction manager a director, who would ask the design office to develop a project, for which, of course, they paid. The approved project would be negotiated by the director with the investor for a twenty percent commission. The investor would then go to the general investor with whom he agreed a forty percent commission and at the same time ask the environmental office for approval. After approval by the authorities, the construction manager would have to certify the hammer with which the worker was going to hammer in the nails. Even before that, the worker would have to get a health card. At the same time, the director of the company would be asked for a solid bribe by lobbyists in the European Commission for approval to use nails corresponding to European standards.

As a result of bureaucracy, corruption and, above all, tactfulness, we have created a unique record in the construction of the highway which is supposed to connect the two largest Slovak cities, Bratislava in the west and Košice in the east. No other European country has such a natural phenomenon. In the thirty-three years since the fall of communism, we've been trying in vain to build the remaining two hundred and fifty kilometres of this highway. From Bratislava to Košice via Žilina, the highway's length is 463 kilometres. 170 kilometres were built under the communists, so 293 remained for the capitalists. According to the information of the National Highway Company, 396 kilometres of this highway are in operation. Since the fall of communism, 396—170 = 226 kilometres have been built. Since communism fell thirty-three years ago, in Slovakia's democratic market system, 226/33 = 6.84 kilometres have been built each year, which amounts to eighteen metres per day. A snail can travel about 130 metres per day, so if snails had built our highways, they would have been eleven times faster. It must be said in public that we could build highways faster, but our traditional tact will not allow us to do so. The faster are more considerate of the slower, the better of the worse, the hardworking of the lazy. I have a friend who says that ambitious people are lazy people who don't have the courage to admit it. My friend is a bartender, and his laziness has really made him famous. His most amazing feat is that he can stand for days with a shaker in his hand and wait for an earthquake. Traditional Slovak tact is manifested in our everyday life.

We are tactful not only towards ourselves, but also towards others. As a result of the ingenious decisions of our largest trading partner, Germany, to withdraw from the production of electricity from coal and nuclear power in the hope that wind and sun will replace coal and nuclear power, a difficult situation in the supply of electricity has also arisen in our country. And this despite the fact that our two nuclear power plants produce so much electricity that we don't know what to do with it, so we sell it to ourselves through the Leipzig stock exchange, but at a five-times higher price than the initial production cost.

Under socialism, we could only dream of such a market economy. Our patriotic government had to react to this situation and, considering Germany's declining energy potential, decided to economize at home. It has introduced many austerity measures to make Germans better off. Ministers come up with some austerity measures on their own and others will be recommended by the European Commission, based on Berlin's recommendation. These recommendations are called guidelines. We like guidelines as we are used to them from the olden days. According to the European directive, the distribution of electricity will also be decentralized, based on the gross domestic product created in individual regions. This is logical, because in an area where less electricity is produced, less is consumed. The government decided that the Prešov region, with the lowest Slovak GDP, will receive electricity with a voltage of 88 volts, while, for example, Trnava has a voltage of 120 volts and Bratislava 240. The decision to supply Bratislava with electricity with almost three times their voltage has created sharp criticism among the citizens of the Prešov region. There have even been cases of some citizens illegally bringing voltage into their homes and secretly storing it in their cellars. Therefore, the Ministry of the Interior has warned citizens that the touch of a greater voltage can seriously shock the user. But citizens cannot be deterred, as they won't do for the suffering Germans, who are allegedly advised by their government to wear thick sweaters and shower in pairs in order to save money.

Our government fulfils the thesis of that great of Marxism-Leninism, Vladimir Ilyich Lenin, who said that even a cook can be the prime minister. I modestly add that the opposite is not true; a prime minister can't be a cook as he would have to know how to cook. However, you don't need to know anything to be the prime minister. Our current Slovak experience clearly demonstrates this. Perhaps this is also the reason why Slovaks continue to be poor despite the promised bright democratic tomorrow. The difference between poverty in a totalitarian regime and a democratic regime is that, while a totalitarian regime creates poverty until it reaches the broad strata of the population, in a democracy wealth is created until the broad strata are affected by poverty. Thanks to the free market in our country, the number of citizens who cannot afford a dentist the day before getting their salary is increasing, so they endure the pain at home with a grinding of teeth.

However, it is not only about teeth, but there is a risk that their ears will also hurt from the ceaseless grinding. There are also people who decide in winter whether to buy medicine or wood for heating. They usually only buy medicines because these are more difficult to steal. This is how we live in our country thirty-three years after the fall of communism; under the old regime, medicine, apartments, education, sports, and culture were almost free. And all this only because we are extremely tactful and kind not only to ourselves as Slovaks, but also to other nations who only wish us well.

Our sixth sorrow is unnecessary tact.

Over the course of my life, I have had the opportunity to talk to people from many nations. Some were closed and taciturn, others open and talkative. They have even participated in a debate with a smile on their faces and with undisguised interest, even if they didn't understand a word, like the Nepalese, Indians or Tibetans. Fortunately, I can communicate in several languages, so I have formed a pretty decent opinion about the way individual nations communicate—and I have discovered an interesting connection. Those peoples who are honest and spontaneous in their communication have a higher standard of living. I have spoken about my books in The Hague, Copenhagen, Vienna, Nicosia, Cairo, Delhi, Prague, Moscow, Warsaw, Budapest, Frankfurt, Zurich and Paris. I have received not just pleasant questions, but people usually express their critical take openly, introducing themselves with their full name. I was a little surprised by this honesty. Slovak friends who have been living in Copenhagen or Amsterdam for a long time explained to me that it took them some time to get used to Dutch or Danish directness. Sometimes they even felt that the Dutch and Danes were impolite when they did not twist and turn their phrasing. After some time, however, they understood that this way of communication is natural to them and they don't want to upset anyone, let alone offend them. My Slovak friend living in the Netherlands confirmed to me that the word anonymous occurs significantly less in that country than in Slovakia. There, the reservations against another are put straight to their face. I have had this experience personally with Nordic peoples and Americans and Canadians. When they have criticized me or publicly opposed me in international forums, I have felt hurt at first, but over time I have come to understand that they meant it sincerely and would consider it dishonourable to express their opinion behind my back. As Christ said, "But let your communication be, Yea, yea; Nay, nay.

Norwegians, Swedes, Danes and Dutch are nations similar in number to Slovaks. It is interesting that they've been able to establish themselves in the world far more than we have. I have thought about their history and ours. Unlike their self-confident histories, we cannot boast about our history. A thousand-year lack of sovereign statehood and thus of responsibility for ourselves reflects our national nature. One day, on one of the staircases in the Vienna Hofburg palace complex, I discovered the inscription "Lakaientreppe", a staircase for lackeys. Our ancestors have ample experience with having served as lackeys. In Vienna, Budapest, but also in our country. Mind you, I mean lackeys and not servants. A servant is one who serves his master devotedly and loves him. A footman is one who pretends to serve his master devotedly, smiles in his eyes, but would rather curse his back. Perhaps the first Slovak Anonymous person was created somewhere here. It seems that the lackey-like tradition of hiding behind anonymity has successfully settled in our genes and is working at full capacity. Many of us have personal experience with Anonymous. Posting in cowardly fashion from the safety of their internet hideouts, they revel in their own stink and get up close and personal with those who cannot defend themselves. They turn head over heels, and when somebody invites them to show their face, when a light is shone onto them, they flee and hide.

I don't know if anonymity, and thus cowardice, has anything to do with it, but I have noticed that life is better where people are more honest. Not only spiritually but also materially. Compare the Protestant countries of Northern Europe with the Catholic ones in the south, which countries act responsibly and which do not, and then compare the standard of living of mostly non-Catholic North America with Catholic South America. I wish I were wrong ...

It is understandable that in a country where the level of pretence and insincerity exceeds the capabilities of the country, laughter is the only possible way to solve problems; thus laughter begins to manifest itself in view of problems. Such experience goes back generations, and suffice it to say that the worse a situation gets, the merrier the people. With regard to humour, we are already ahead of even the most laughter-prone foreign countries. For example, the Norwegian Stoltenberg, head of the otherwise mostly serious NATO organization, showed a great sense of humour when he declared that NATO cannot be drawn into an arms race with Russia, because NATO produces twenty-five times more weapons than Russia. Fortunately, our government is already catching up with this humourist at the head of NATO. Maybe I can take modest credit for it. Some time ago, I told a member of the government that if I had a sense of humour like his, I would become an undertaker to make a living. The member of the government in question became famous for his enthusiastic telling of anecdotes about cinema, with which he consistently prolonged the sessions of our governing body. When he was heard saying "And do you know this one?", some members of the government pulled out their newspapers, and the weaker crawled under the table. However, the humorous minister wouldn't give up.

"He meets someone else and asks him: 'Where are you going?'"

"To the cinema"

"What is playing?"

"Quo vadis?"

"What does that mean?"

"Where are you going?"

"To the cinema."

"What's playing?"

"Quo vadis?"

"What does that mean?"

When the minister realized that his colleagues were not laughing, he began to explain: "Don't you understand? The punchline is Quo vadis? In Latin it means 'where are you going?' So when he asked what was playing and the other answered 'Quo vadis?' he was actually saying, where are you going? Do you understand now?" This was usually the moment when the members of the government burst into fits of laughter. At first, I was sorry that this man had already left politics. Fortunately, he was replaced by fresh humourists. For example, we have the only finance minister in the world who honestly admitted that he doesn't understand finances and that his wife handles the finances in their family as well. However, he became the first Slovak in history to have an umbrella held over his head by the French president. That was at a time when this minister was still prime minister. It turned out that he doesn't meet the basic criteria for a Slovak, who is usually born with a brain. Unfortunately, the fact that he doesn't have one in his head only came to light when he became prime minister. He's doing relatively well in his position as Minister of Finance because he has yet to realize that he has no brain. Well, but how else should he figure it out ... However, he is convinced that he belongs to those Slovaks who have a sense of humour. Statistics prove that there are more and more people from our country with a sense of humour. In the days of the communist dictatorship, 46.4 percent of citizens in Slovakia had a sense of humour, who demonstrated this sense with the words, "What's left, we won't change anyway." Today, 46.4 percent of citizens in Slovakia have a sense of humour, who demonstrate this sense with the words "What remains to us, we will not change anything about things anyway."

So, **the seventh sorrow** that hurts Slovakia is too much humour.

However, it seems to me that, unlike Slovakia, there is less and less laughter in our lovely Europe. So, at the end of my reflections on Slovakia's sins or sorrows, I allow myself to dream a little about the sins of our Europe. Or her hopes? Just as Martin Luther King once dreamt his American dream, I dream my European dream. I dream of a Europe of happy people who care about full hearts more than full fists, who try to love their neighbour more than themselves, who unconditionally respect God's law: "Give, and it shall be given unto you." I dream of a Europe in which we do not pursue endless growth of the gross national product just so that we can pay interest to greedy banks, due to which we mercilessly destroy nature and the future of our children. I dream of a Europe where work will be a joyful activity for people and not a grind for daily bread, where we will form a community of free and equal people and not a manipulated and amorphous mass, whose only task is to consume, toil, and give birth to new consumers and workers. I dream of a Europe that isn't driven by consumerism, where a two-hour film lasts two hours on television and not four, because it is just a vehicle for increasingly aggressive advertising, where people go to their pub after work, drink wine and sing together.

I dream of a Europe in which we eat eggs from hens that run on the grass and do not die in cages, where milk doesn't turn mouldy the next day but turns sour like it used to. I dream of a Europe whose peoples will enrich each other with the fruits of their culture and education and not homogenize into a uniform grey, dead, globalized mass, where culture won't be considered a commodity subject to the rules of free trade. I dream of a Europe where I shall be able to watch not only Hollywood productions in the cinema, but also Wajda, Tarkowski, Bergmann, Fassbinder, Jancsó, Menzel, Tarantino or Szabó, where we shall value nations according to the fire in their souls and not according to the firepower of their guns.

I dream of a Europe where we still have peasants and not farmers, where there is news on TV and not headlines, where we honour national traditions and not the traditions of Halloween and Valentine's Day, where people talk on the train and don't look at each other with empty eyes with headphones on their ears, where we sit in a café in order to spend pleasant moments with friends who are there, and not to have to text friends who are absent, where neighbours know and greet each other, where people live in solidarity and help each other, where we welcome a stranger with open arms because we invited him and not because the stranger invades our home and occupies our bed. I dream of a Europe that real leaders lead and not officials willing to spend their lives bowing to the powerful from across the Atlantic for a warm place, where the word journalist and politician inspires respect and not contempt. I dream of media that will inform us and not manipulate us; media that, together with us, the citizens, will search for the truth and not lie. I dream of a Europe in which the French will join hands with the English, the English with the German and the German with the Russian for the sake of stability, prosperity and peace. I believe in a Europe where the fish smells from the head and doesn't stink, where political elites will be moral examples for their people. I dream of courageous European women and men who, just as they found the courage to send the fossils of Moscow into oblivion, will also send the fossils of Brussels into oblivion. They who have sown the wind shall also reap the whirlwind, for such is God's law. Earthly laws can be fled from, but not God's. I dream of a Europe where the only criterion for the development of each individual will not be the effort to be better than the others, but that each of us will try to be better today than he was yesterday. I dream of a future in which we will stop looking for the mote in our neighbour's eye and remove the beam from our own eye.

This is the European dream of a Slovak writer. This dream isn't what we dream when we sleep, but what keeps us awake. I can't sleep because of the seven sorrows of Slovakia, I'm afraid that they won't rub off on Europe. If that happened, it would be a problem. For Europe, not for us. We already have a patron saint, the Virgin Mary of the Seven Sorrows, who will protect us. But who will protect Europe?

Index

ibidem.eu